The Key to His Heart

Unlocking God's Heart for One
Church, One Body—and One Bride

Ever More
&
Ever Deeper
♡ Karin

Cindy Powell

Cover art by Aeron Brown: www.aeronbrown.com

Published by Simple Faith Press: P.O. Box 345, Redlands, CA 92373

All Scripture quotations, unless otherwise indicated, are taken from the Holy Bible: New International Version®. NIV®.

ISBN-13: 978-0615683881 (Simple Faith Press)
ISBN-10: 0615683886

To the hungry ones.

"Blessed are those who hunger and thirst for righteousness, for they will be filled."

CONTENTS

Acknowledgements — 1

Preface — 3

Introduction: The Key to His Heart — 5

I. **The Time Has Come:** Hearts Prepared for Change — 9

Chapter 1 Time for Change! — 10

Chapter 2 Love, the Agent of Change — 18

Chapter 3 That We May Know Him — 28

Chapter 4 The Need for Endurance — 39

II. **Revealing the Father:** Hearts Aligned with His — 51

Chapter 5 Jesus = Perfect Theology — 52

Chapter 6 The Power of His Name — 63

Chapter 7 The Power of Identity — 74

Chapter 8 Remembering the Forgotten — 85

Chapter 9 Fullness of Joy — 97

Chapter 10 Sent Into the World — 108

III. **For All Who Will Believe:** Hearts Beating as One — 119

Chapter 11 Israel, the Master Key — 120

Chapter 12 The Big Picture — 132

Chapter 13 That All of Them May Be One — 142

Chapter 14 The Cost and Reward of Unity — 154

IV. **Continuing to Make Him Known** — 167

ACKNOWLEDGMENTS

Since we function best together, it is impossible for one person to accomplish much of anything without a lot of help from the body. This project is no exception. First and foremost, I need to thank everyone who prayed and encouraged me along the way. Many dear friends have done this for years; others God brought along at strategic intersections. There are too many to name, but I hope you all know who you are! Special thanks to Andrea and Karin because without the two of you, this manuscript may not have left my computer! Ty, thanks for your time, encouragement, and help with wandering commas. Aeron, your art is always amazing. Even more — your heart of passion for Jesus is amazing.

I am eternally grateful for the ministry of the International House of Prayer in Kansas City, MO. The first time I walked into the prayer room, I knew I had finally found "my people" and a place where I fit. This book would not exist without the sanctuary and stirring I find there. Closer to home, Ted and Toni, thank you for giving me the keys to the building! The Refuge was just that (and so much more) at a time I desperately needed one. Thankful also for my spiritual communities at both CCF and the Acts Center. Fraser and Jo Anne, thank you for welcoming and accepting me for who I *am*, rather than what I could *do*. Kevin and Lorna, what a joy it is to be part of what God is doing in our region — so privileged and excited to run with you! Dave and Becky, thank you for going out of your way for me and for modeling true love and acceptance with your actions and not just words. You saw me at my most broken and vulnerable, but I never had to be guarded. Thank you for believing in me.

I am also so very grateful for my family. Mom, you believed this thing I do with words was a gift long before I did. I love you. To my amazing son and daughter-in-law, and my beautiful daughter — I love you and I'm so very proud of you. You fill me with such hope for your generation.

And finally, all thanks and praise to the One who knows each beat of my heart. Jesus, you've completely wrecked me with your love and I've never been more glad. I've never regretted a single moment I've given to you — never, not one. My desire above all is that the life you've given me will be poured out as an offering for the sake of the dream you carry in your heart. At long last, *"May the Lamb that was slain receive the reward of his suffering!"*

PREFACE

$\mathcal{G}$ began writing the introduction to this book several years ago while on a plane en route to Los Angeles from Tel Aviv. I had spent the previous several weeks in Jerusalem on one of the greatest adventures of my life. Over and over again during my time in Israel the Holy Spirit had exhorted me to *"Write the vision and make it plain"* (Hab. 2:2). I knew the Lord wanted me to write down the things he had been showing me in a way that was simple and accessible. I wanted to be faithful, so of course I couldn't wait to start!

Well, I didn't get very far. I had a title and managed to write a few paragraphs, but that's as far as I got. Although things were stirring in my heart, they hadn't quite made it to my head! Before I could share anything with anyone else, I needed time to gain greater understanding *myself* first. It's taken a lot longer than I would have guessed, but I have finally come to a place where I feel compelled to share the things that have been percolating in my heart for years. This is my attempt to do so.

I tend to write from the heart to the heart. While John 17 provides the (very loose) framework for this book, this is *not* –

in any way, shape, or form — intended to be a formal study of John 17. I am not a theologian and I am not writing from a theological perspective. What I am is a simple person who loves Jesus — and I know that *he* loves his Church.

I have been quite vulnerable throughout these pages by sharing some rather deep and intimate details of my own journey with Jesus. I have also shared a few profound and life changing encounters. My purpose and prayer in revealing these details is simple: I want to stir hunger and longing in the hearts of the reader. Not necessarily a hunger for the *same kind* of experiences but rather *a hunger to press into his heart*. We are all wired differently, so a deeper revelation of God's heart may look very different to you than it does to me. This is the beauty of being one body with many parts.

Throughout this manuscript, I have capitalized "Church" when referring to the global Body of Christ; when referring to a smaller or more localized group of believers, I have simply used "church".

Finally, and perhaps most importantly, this is *not* a "how-to" book. I am keenly aware that the topic being addressed is far more complex and multi-dimensional than the scope of this manuscript. I do not profess to have a "plan" for moving the Church into alignment with God's heart. While there may be a practical tip or two along the way, more than anything, my desire is to simply draw attention to *his* desires (as I understand them). Really, this book is about a journey — our journey with him and our journey with each other. Along the way, my prayer is that you will discover more about who you are, whose you are — and how Jesus would have *you* respond.

INTRODUCTION:
The Key to His Heart

*I*t was a Sunday afternoon about six years ago, but I remember it like it was yesterday. I had the afternoon free and allowed myself the luxury of lying down to take little nap. I never went to sleep. Instead, the presence of God surrounded me and enveloped me like a cloud. I didn't know it at the time, but I was about to embark upon a journey that would forever change the course of my life.

The familiar surroundings of my bedroom faded and I had the sensation of being propelled into another dimension. I soon realized Jesus had literally taken me deep into the center of his own heart. I could actually hear and feel the heartbeat of heaven. All of creation, *every* living thing, beat in perfect unity to a single rhythm — the rhythm of his heart.

I don't possess language to adequately express what I saw and heard that day. Even carefully chosen words are able to convey only a shadow of the beauty and wonder I was privileged to glimpse. I can only hope his Spirit will somehow communicate what my own words fail to capture.

In harmony with the beating of his heart, I heard the Lord's voice resounding throughout creation. His cry contained inexpressible depths of joy, passion, and anguish all at the same time, as he exclaimed over and over again: *That they may be one! That they may be one!*

As he declared his heart's desire, I began to see the Bride of Christ emerge in the reflection of his glory. She began walking toward him and as she did, she grew in strength and beauty with each step. Somehow, a map of the globe—every tribe, every tongue, and every nation represented—was superimposed upon her. She was radiant! I could *feel* the joy and anticipation in his heart as she approached him. His heart was literally bursting with love and longing.

It ended too quickly. But while I was still, as the Apostle John would say, "in the spirit" the Lord had one more thing to impart. He asked me to stretch out my hand. As I did, he placed a key in the center of my palm. When I asked him what it was, his response was simple: *It's the key to my heart.*

God often speaks very simply, but even when he does, the depth of what he is communicating tends to lie beyond our current comprehension. He loves it when we pursue him for greater revelation. Personally, I think he likes the thrill of the chase! From the moment the Lord gave me the precious gift of this encounter, I set my heart toward gaining greater wisdom and revelation in its application. It has taken me these past several years of praying and pondering to gain greater insight into understanding the profound simplicity of what he shared: The key to his heart lies in grasping the depth of his longing for *one* "pure spotless bride." We are that bride—made pure and spotless by the cleansing of his blood—but we are not yet one.

Long before the Lord revealed this glimpse of his heart, the strange subject of "unity" in the Church had frequently perplexed and saddened me. For the most part we can't even agree on what it should look like, let alone how to walk it out. The words I heard the Lord speak, *"That they may be one"* are from Jesus' prayer in John 17. He recently drew my attention back to this amazing passage of Scripture to consider his words further. I believe this chapter holds not only the key to *his* heart, but also the keys the Church must apprehend in order to ultimately *"be brought to complete unity"* (John 17:23).

I am convinced it is only within the context of "oneness" with Jesus that we will begin to understand an authentic expression of unity with each other. Paul expresses this concept in his letter to the Ephesians: *From him the whole body, joined and held together by every supporting ligament, grows and builds itself up in love, as each part does its work* (Eph. 4:16). Paul describes a healthy body, *rightly related to the Head* (to Christ), functioning properly with each part doing its own assigned work, growing and being built up in love. Sadly, I have not known this to describe the reality of the Church. I'm not okay with that and you shouldn't be either.

Starting nearly two decades ago, when I organized a small prayer group at my place of employment that reached across multiple denominational lines and church traditions, I have participated in various non-denominational and cross-denominational ministries and prayer groups. I have been in partnership with churches that have differed dramatically in their vision and values. I have been privileged to visit churches of almost every shape, size, and variety—literally around the globe—and I have worked for large ministries that have served both the local and global Church. All of these experiences have given me a fairly broad glimpse into the heartbeat of the mysterious organism we call the Body of Christ. Although there have been many glorious glimmers of love, life, and hope, far too often I have been deeply grieved by what I've witnessed and experienced. We are many things, but we are not yet one — not with him, not within ourselves, and certainly not with each other.

In many areas — particularly in the West — the body is sleepy, sick, and broken. There are "parts" that seem to function better than others, but we are not even close to functioning *in the whole* as the healthy, mutually supportive system that Paul describes in Ephesians 4. And without the whole, even the parts that seem to function better are only functioning at a fraction of their intended purpose and potential. I suspect it is similar to being sick your entire life — you become so used to being sick that you don't have any idea what it would feel like to be healthy and whole.

I believe God is highlighting this issue in this hour because he is positioning us for healing and change. We were created and designed to function as one Church, one body, and, ultimately, one bride. We need each other. Far more importantly, it is Jesus' own desire that we be "brought to complete unity." It's what he prayed for and it's what he bought with his own blood. I, for one, want him to have what it cost him so dearly to purchase. My fervent prayer and heart's desire is that a fire will be stirred within the hearts of God's people that will take us one step closer to that reality, until, at last, our cry echo's his own:

That we may be one! That we may be one!

I. "THE TIME HAS COME"

Hearts Prepared for Change

"Father, the time has come: Glorify your Son, that your Son may glorify you." **–John 17:1**

When Jesus said, *"Father, the time has come,"* a shift was already taking place. There is a shift taking place in the Church today as well. Jesus was ready for the journey ahead of him and *we* need to be ready for the journey ahead of us. In the amazing prayer recorded in John 17, Jesus prayed first for himself. He was fixing his eyes and his heart on the prize. If Jesus needed to prepare *his* heart for what was ahead, we can be certain we need to do the same. Change will come whether we embrace it or not, but when our hearts are prepared — when our priorities and commitment to finishing the race are firmly established — we can look ahead with joy, confidence, and perseverance.

Father, the time has come. Please open our hearts to embrace your plans for the Church in this hour. Prepare our hearts for all you desire to do in us and through us, that we might bring you great glory on the earth!

CHAPTER 1

Time for Change!

*I*n the beginning, God had the end in mind. Even before the Garden of Eden, God knew there would be a cross — but he also knew there would be a wedding.

Like many churches in the weeks approaching Christmas, my church celebrates Advent. Last year during each of our Sunday services in December, a different young person from the congregation was invited to briefly share their personal understanding of that particular week's Advent theme. When the theme was joy, a young woman named Rebecca got up to speak. She relayed that she had been a little perplexed when she first started seeking the Lord on the subject of joy. Every time she did, all she could think about was the cross. That wasn't exactly what she expected! When Rebecca "reminded" the Lord that this was, after all, Christmas and *not* Easter, she heard him speak to her very clearly: *You can't separate the end from the beginning.*

In life there are many seasons and through them all God always has the end in mind. Change is all around us, all the time. Some change is forced on us, some change we choose. There are many beginnings, many endings, and then more beginnings. It is the cycle of life. In the midst of this cycle, it is important to remember there *is* an ultimate purpose in it all. *This is going somewhere.* There *is* an ultimate ending ahead that will finally lead to the ultimate beginning — the beginning that will never end.

Paradigm Shifts of the Past

When Jesus prayed his beautiful prayer in John 17, his earthly ministry was about to end. At the same time, the ministry of the Church was just about to begin. Since the birth of the Church over two thousand years ago, there have been many key seasons of transition and change throughout the body. I believe we are in the midst of another of those key seasons.

Although most of us don't spend a tremendous amount of time pondering the significant transitions or paradigm shifts of the past, we all owe a great debt to those who went before us and plowed hard ground to reclaim truths that had been lost to the Church as a whole. For example, consider the doctrine of salvation as a gift of God's grace. When I turned to Jesus with my whole heart, I *knew* that I belonged to him. I can honestly say that since I made a conscious choice to accept his gift of forgiveness and eternal life, I have never doubted my salvation. When I take my last breath on this planet — I know that I know that I *know* — I will live forever in his presence. I am so completely convinced of this reality that I honestly don't know if there is anything that could persuade me otherwise. Like countless others, I have personally experienced the truth of Romans 8:16, *"The Spirit Himself bears witness with our spirit that we are children of God"* (NKJV).

I simply believed and walked right through an open door of grace to lay hold of a gift that had already been purchased for me. However, just five hundred years or so earlier, *that assurance would have been nearly unthinkable.* Although the Church started out with a keen understanding that salvation is a gift of grace that can only be received by faith, somewhere along the way this foundational truth was stripped away. Since access to God's Word was limited and distorted, a veil settled over the hearts and minds of God's people and blinded them to the goodness of his grace. Fortunately God's eyes are always searching for those who will hear his heart and restore truth to his people. He found such a man in a monk named Martin Luther.

In October of 1517, Martin Luther posted his 95 theses on the door of the church in Wittenberg and set off a chain of events that ultimately restored the doctrine of salvation by grace through faith to any and all with ears to hear. It was not an easy or quick process. It did not happen seamlessly or perfectly. It came at a huge cost, including great persecution. An incredibly significant battle was won, but many others— including an enormous splintering of the Church—had just begun. Martin Luther, like all of us, was not a perfect man and some of his ideas are rejected by many in the Church today. However, even those who are not in complete agreement with all of his doctrine *are still able to enjoy the fruit of his labor.*

To put it another way, Martin Luther and other reformers "pierced a veil" in the heavenly realms. They battled hard against the widely accepted ideology of the day to lay hold of a truth that was always ours but had been lost through neglect, unbelief, and the agenda of hell to "kill, steal, and destroy" (John 10:10). Now that this particular truth has been restored in much of the Church, literally millions around the globe have confidence in the reality of their salvation.

This is only one example of a key shift in the history of the Church. Another more recent example occurred in California around the turn of the century with the Azusa Street Revival. Thanks to the earnest seeking and unrelenting prayers of William Seymour and others, the Holy Spirit was poured out and made his presence and power known to a Church that had nearly forgotten his existence. As a result, today there are more than 500 million Pentecostal and charismatic believers around the globe and it the fastest growing Christian movement in the world today. Virtually all Pentecostal denominations, as well as major "non-denominational" charismatic movements such as Calvary Chapel and Vineyard, can trace their roots directly to Azusa Street.

Since this "promise of the Father" (Acts 1:4-5) was reclaimed, multitudes around the globe have been able to enter into fellowship with the Holy Spirit with greater ease and confidence thanks to those of a previous generation who contended persistently until they laid hold of the promise. Now *we* have the privilege of simply believing and walking into the fruit of their labor. The Scriptures regarding the gifts and power of the Holy Spirit didn't change — *but a large scale corporate understanding of these Scriptures did.*

In the same way, there are many passages of Scripture that describe the unity of the saints; many Scriptures that describe a healthy, optimally functioning Body of Christ; and many Scriptures that describe God's longing for one pure spotless bride. The Scriptures themselves will never change, but I believe our understanding of them is about to change dramatically.

Following the Cloud

When Jesus entered this world the first time, *God* did absolutely nothing the way we would have expected or planned, yet he perfectly fulfilled *every* prophecy concerning his coming. All the pieces were there. All the prophecies that foretold his coming were precise and accurate, yet no one put all those pieces together and fully apprehended the enormity, and even absurdity, of his plan. Come on—*seriously*—God in a manger? The Creator himself taking on human flesh? A helpless baby born to a poor teenager in a stinky cave used by livestock in a small, forgotten town? Who could have guessed? Yet it was all foretold. Every promise, every prophecy was fulfilled perfectly, but it all looked so different than anything anyone could have imagined.

I think God likes it that way. Things usually don't look the way we think they should look and they rarely happen how, or when, we think they should happen. Yet the Lord always fulfills his Word perfectly.

God is not limited by our current understanding, nor is he subject to our methods and timetables. Many missed Jesus the first time around because he didn't look the way they thought he should look, and he didn't come how and when they thought he should come. It's frightening to think he could be right in front of us and we could completely miss what he is doing. Yet if we insist on stubbornly clinging to our own ideas and ideals, and if we refuse to move beyond the pseudo-safety of our current understanding, "missing him" is an all too real possibility.

Not everyone missed Jesus the first time around and we don't need to miss him now. Those with eyes to see and ears to hear—did see and did hear. Like Moses and the Israelites in the wilderness, we need to be ready to simply follow the cloud. When he moves, we need to move. Our hearts need to be alert, awake, and open to his leading—now more than ever.

Some years ago, I was part of a large church that outgrew its current facility. Additional land was purchased on an adjacent lot and construction of a new, much larger building began. Originally the building was scheduled to be completed by early December, but delays were encountered and it seemed the final move-in date would be no sooner than January. Ultimately the new building was completed before Christmas, but there still needed to be a final inspection so we didn't expect to actually hold services there until after the holidays.

I was glad. I knew the new building was a good thing. God was blessing the church and we needed more room. But I also liked the old building. It was familiar. It was comfortable. And I had a lot of wonderful memories attached to it. I was sorry the building project had been delayed, but I was very grateful to have one final Christmas Eve service in our comfy, cozy old sanctuary. The Christmas Eve services there had always been especially warm and intimate. Then the cloud moved.

When I showed up on Christmas Eve, the lights were out in the old building and on in the new one. The city had granted a special permit to allow the service to be held in the new building. It was a surprise for most of the congregation. It certainly was a surprise for me — a rather traumatic one! I went expecting to have a final "moment" in the familiar surroundings of our old sanctuary and was instead thrust into completely new territory.

Often that is how change goes. Often that is how *life* goes. His ways are not our ways. Even when we *do* expect change, sometimes we'd like just a bit more time to adjust; a bit more time to prepare. We don't always have that luxury. When the cloud moves, we need to simply get up follow — without looking back.

Taking New Ground

In the overall scheme of things changing church buildings is a minor thing, but even in that relatively small adjustment I knew I had a choice. I could resist the change or get up and follow the cloud. All change involves a choice. We can lean into what God is doing and partner with him wherever he leads, or we can stubbornly hold onto old ground. The problem with refusing to move when God moves is that you never take *new* ground. And if you are never willing to take new ground — eventually you get left behind.

The call of Abraham in Genesis 12:1 is a familiar story to many: *"The LORD had said to Abram, 'Leave your country, your people and your father's household and go to the land I will show you.'"* That land, of course, was Canaan and Abraham did go. But what about Abraham's father, Terah? In Genesis 11:31 we read, *"Terah took his son Abram, his grandson Lot son of Haran, and his daughter-in-law Sarai, the wife of his son Abram, and together they set out from Ur of the Chaldeans to go to Canaan. But when they came to Haran, they settled there."*

Could it be that the original call to go to Canaan went not to Abraham, but to his father, Terah? Of course Scripture doesn't specifically say that God told Terah to go to Canaan, but it *does* specifically say that Terah set out *for Canaan* but "settled" in Haran — about halfway there. The next verse is even more troubling, *"And he (Terah) died in Haran."* Terah never made it to his final destination. He settled halfway to Canaan and never went any farther.

If we're not willing to move when God moves — if we're not willing to change when the seasons change — it *is* possible to be left out of God's plans. It is possible to say, "I'll go this far and no farther." *"Remember Lot's wife!"* (Luke 17:32). This was Jesus' exhortation to those at the end of the age. Lot's wife looked back and missed what God was doing in front of her. She was given the opportunity to be a part of what God was doing in the future and instead became a monument to the past. God will never violate our free will, if we want to stay in the past, he won't drag us kicking and screaming into the future. But he is always looking for someone who *will* listen. He is always looking someone who *will* move with him into the future. He is always looking for someone who *will* follow him all the way. I pray he finds a lot of those "someone's" in this generation.

There is land to be taken. The time is at hand. Change is coming. God always has the end in mind—and so should we. We need to remember this *is* going somewhere. But before we reach the ultimate end, there is spiritual ground that must be reclaimed and a shift that must take place. There are promises that have yet to be apprehended. To lay hold of them we will need to move with the Holy Spirit into new territory. We will need to follow the Lamb wherever he goes. We will need to embrace change.

Often change *is* painful. It costs something. I've heard it said that we are willing to change when the pain of staying the same is greater than the pain of change. For me—and for many others—the pain of remaining the same has simply become too great. When you are gripped by the heartbeat of heaven, staying the same is no longer an option. May we burn with the desire to move where he moves and do what he does …

"Until we all reach unity in the faith and in the knowledge of the Son of God and become mature, attaining to the whole measure of fullness of Christ." **–Eph. 4:13**

CHAPTER 2

Love, the Agent of Change

$\mathscr{I}$ still affectionately refer to it as the day God yelled at me.
Although I had been a believer of sorts from the time I was very young, I didn't have a true revelation of Jesus until I was in my early thirties. Prior to that, I believed as much as I understood. The problem is that I didn't understand much — least of all his love.

Immediately after my eyes were open to the reality of Jesus as both my Savior *and* Lord, I determined to seek after him with all of my heart and soul and strength. It was during this early stage of seeking to truly *know* him that I had an experience that marked me for life.

It was not difficult for me to set apart quiet time to spend with the Lord each day. Even though I was an extremely busy working single mother, I loved getting up early to start my day alone with him. I was literally devouring his Word during this season. I understood so little before, I wanted to learn as much as I could as quickly as I could. Spending time in prayer was also relatively easy for me. I had been engaged in an ongoing conversation with God since I was a small child, but up to that point it had mostly been a monologue. I never thought he was all that interested in talking to me.

I was wrong.

As far as I can remember, my time with Jesus that day started out like any other, but it didn't end that way. I began by simply thanking him for all he was doing in my life. That in itself wasn't unusual, but on this particular day I became completely overwhelmed with gratitude. Something shifted in a tangible way and I experienced a very profound sense of his presence. I entered into a transcendent sort of place where time ceased to exist. There was only him — and me with him.

I don't know how long I was in this place of worship and communion — I just knew I never wanted to leave. For the very first time I caught a glimpse of the timelessness of eternity. I knew that *this* I could do forever.

Eventually the sense of his presence lifted a bit and I realized I needed to pay attention to the business of daily life and get ready for work. But I didn't want to leave. I was so drawn to him and had such a deep longing to simply be with him that I literally had to pull myself away. As I did — with the eyes of my heart — I saw a very clear picture of Jesus' face. He was weeping. But I knew instantly they weren't tears of sorrow, they were tears of joy! He was absolutely overwhelmed with joy that I *wanted* to be with him so much.

I no sooner absorbed this beautiful sight than my old nature and old thought patterns began to emerge. The internal dialogue went something like this: *Yeah, right! Like God really cares about you that much. Get real!*

And that's when it happened. I have never heard the external audible voice of God, but this had to be awfully close!

His voice literally boomed within my spirit with a thundering "NO!" that shook me to the core of my being. He certainly had my attention. Now that I was listening, his message was simple:

You need to believe I love you that much, because it's my love that will change you.

Although I heard him loud and clear, I had no idea how profoundly true those words would prove to be. I have been on a journey of learning the transforming way of Love ever since.

Love that Surpasses Knowledge

Many of us would say we know God loves us. After all, he is God and loving us is pretty much a part of his job description. God *is* love (1 John 4:8). Around the globe, one of the best known verses in the Bible is John 3:16, *"For God so loved the world...."* If God loves the world, by default that must mean he loves *me*. Anyone with at least a basic understanding of the cross can't help but grasp, at some level, the enormity of God's love for mankind. The problem isn't a lack of head knowledge—it is a lack of *heart* knowledge. Many people acknowledge God's love on an intellectual level *but they don't know it personally on an experiential level.* They don't know it in their "knower."

It has been scientifically proven that we learn quickest through experiences that engage our emotions. Yet much of the western church has become so afraid of falling into emotional excess that we often find it safer to keep our faith on a strictly intellectual plane. Although many conversions involve some level of emotional experience, our intellect takes over from there. We are taught that it demonstrates a lack of faith to desire ongoing manifestations of God's affections. It is true that *how* he reveals his love to us may change as we mature, but we never outgrow our need to *experience* God's love.

In the book of Ephesians, Paul prays that we might *"grasp how wide and long and high and deep is the love of Christ, and to know this love that surpasses knowledge"* (Eph. 3:18-19). The word translated "know" is the Greek word "ginosko." The word implies a knowledge that comes from intimate, personal experience—a "felt" knowledge. Paul is not speaking of intellectually acknowledging the love of God; he is speaking of personally *knowing* the love of God in a way that goes far beyond natural intellect and understanding.

After "the day God yelled at me" I set out on a mission to *know* the love of God. I would pray, over and over again, to "know it in my knower." I don't know exactly when it happened, but somewhere along the way it *did* happen. Oh boy did it happen! There are many things I struggle with, but knowing God loves me is *not* one of them. Somehow I became convinced that he not only loves me—he *likes* me. He delights in me. He rejoices over me. *He enjoys being with me.* He sings and dances over me, and sometimes I even sing and dance with him. I am convinced he thinks I'm exceptionally special. He paints sunsets for me and he even gave me my own star. He would have created the entire universe just for me. In fact, I'm *firmly* convinced that I'm his all-time favorite!

Misty Edwards, a worship leader at the International House of Prayer in Kansas City, Missouri, seems to think she is God's favorite too. In her song "Favorite One" she sings: *Jesus, here I am your favorite one. What are you thinking? What are you feeling? I have to know.* A friend shared with me that she was bothered by the lyrics the first time she heard the song. She couldn't even sing the words because she thought the whole idea was just a tad arrogant! But when she talked to the Lord about it, Jesus made it quite clear that *he* didn't share her opinion. Instead he responded that the lyrics represented the heart of one *who knew who she was to him*. Really, they are the expression of a heart that *knows* the love of God.

My friend isn't the only one who has struggled with the idea of being God's favorite. Many believers are very uncomfortable discussing how much God loves them *personally*. More than once, I've heard some particularly sincere servant of the Lord point out that this line of thinking is an exercise in self-absorption. After all, shouldn't our eyes be on God and others—*not* ourselves? Well yes ... and no.

It is impossible to give away what you don't have. We need to keep receiving his love to keep giving it away. My love has limits. My love keeps score. My love wears out, but his never does. His love knows no bounds. The more you know the love of God for yourself—the more secure you are in his love—the more you can authentically and unselfishly give it away.

A Beautiful "Waste"

As I came to know God's love for myself, I grew in the great pleasure of loving him and being loved by him. I enjoyed simply being with him so much that I often thought I must be doing something wrong. Almost all of the messages I heard during this season of life were about "do, do, doing." Whether it was the practice of spiritual disciplines or performing acts of service—or both—the focus always seemed to be on doing more rather than on simply seeking God's heart.

Initially, this conflict of priorities caused me much confusion. Although I sincerely desired to love and serve Jesus with my whole life, I constantly carried a burden that somehow I wasn't doing enough. Since I was more interested in spending time with him than I was in participating in every possible ministry opportunity, I was sure I must be horribly lazy or selfish — or both. Once again, God revealed a different opinion in the matter.

It started nearly fifteen years ago when I left my home church and several ministries that had been a big part of my life to move to a completely new area. I was confident the Lord knew my desire to serve him and I believed he would open the right doors at the right time for new areas of ministry. Well, he *did* open the right doors at the right time, but let's just say they weren't necessarily the doors I'd envisioned! After running into more brick walls than open doors, my perception of "ministry" slowly began to change. As it did, I found contentment in a few quiet and not so visible areas of service. However, just a few short years later he made it quite clear I was to step out of those areas as well.

Since the Lord made it so obvious it was time to lay down those things, that's what I did. During this same period, my times in the "secret place" with Jesus took on a new dimension. With more frequency and intensity than ever before, I was drawn into a deep and intimate place of communion with him. I was often so overwhelmed by his presence that I couldn't even speak, let alone pray. Over and over again, I was completely lost in love and worship.

I was so blessed by these times and so wooed by his Spirit that I didn't do much to resist. Although I cherished each moment, deep in my heart I was still uneasy. I felt guilty. I thought I was spending way too much time getting "blessed" and not nearly enough time praying for others. Even when I had no other visible ministry, I knew I could pray. Since there were always so many needs to consider, was I wasting my prayer time selfishly pursuing my own fulfillment?

God's response came by way of a familiar passage in the Gospel of Matthew:

While Jesus was in Bethany in the home of a man known as Simon the Leper, a woman came to him with an alabaster jar of very expensive perfume, which she poured on his head as he was reclining at the table. When the disciples saw this, they were indignant. "Why this waste?" they asked. "This perfume could have been sold at a high price and giving to the poor." Aware of this, Jesus said to them, "Why are you bothering this woman? She has done a beautiful thing to me. The poor you will always have with you, but you will not always have me." **–Matt.26:6-13**

The words, "Why this waste?" pierced my heart like a knife. That had been *my* attitude. I thought my time would have been better spent in what I considered to be more noble service to others. Truthfully, I realized I *was* being selfish, but not in the way I had thought. It wasn't the needs of others I wasn't considering — *it was the heart of God I wasn't considering.* I was so focused on how being with him blessed *me*, it rarely occurred to me how much it blessed *him*. I was so anxious to be of "use" to him that I almost missed the highest call of all. In simply loving him, being with him, and responding to his presence in worship, I *was* serving him — in the very purest sense.

There will always be more needs than we can ever hope to meet. We can only meet the needs he calls us to meet, when and how he calls and equips us to meet them. But when we fail to lay hold of those precious moments with him — those moments of loving him and allowing him the joy of lavishing his love on us — we miss his heartbeat. We miss the point. The point is simply this: We were made for love. And only love has the power to transform.

Loving As He Loves Us

As we are transformed in the very presence of Love, our relationships with others are eventually transformed as we begin to *walk out* the reality of his love in our daily lives and interactions with others. Some people are easy to love, but as Jesus said, *"If you love only those who love you, what reward will you get?"* (Matt. 5:46). In other words, what eternal benefit is there in loving only those we are naturally predisposed to love? But when we become secure enough in his love to genuinely love our enemies—or simply those with whom we have conflict and disagreement—we enter into a supernatural and transformational reality.

We all have "prickly" people in our lives; those special people who just seem to have a knack for getting on every single nerve. One of the prickliest people in my life—I'll call her Ann—was part of a prayer ministry I served with. Ann sincerely loved Jesus but she had extremely strong opinions that made many, if not all, of her interpersonal relationships very, very difficult.

Even though she made me crazy at times, somehow Jesus enabled me to see her heart. There were times I would be *so* mad at her, but then I'd pray—more to shake the anger off myself than to pray for her!—and over and over again it seemed as if God's own heart would take over and I'd find myself weeping tender tears of mercy for her. I truly grew to love her.

One day she did something in front of several other people that was *not* okay in any way, shape, or form. It was so incredibly inappropriate that I knew I would need to say something to her. I was not looking forward to it.

Apparently neither was Ann. She obviously knew I wanted to talk to her and didn't want anything to do with me. As soon as the last person left the prayer room that evening, she got up and high-tailed it out so quickly it made my head spin. With uncharacteristic boldness, I jumped up and ran after her. Since she kept trying to avoid me, I managed to position myself in such a way that I actually blocked her exit route! She was *not* happy. Before I could say a word, she let me have it with both barrels. Thankfully, I have absolutely no recollection of what she specifically said, but it seemed to be a litany of all the wrongs I had ever committed in her eyes—both real and imagined. When she finally took a breath, I looked straight into her eyes and simply said, "I love you." Then she started in on me again. When, at last, she took another breath, again I looked straight at her and said, "I love you."

This went on for one more round. By the third time something strange and miraculous happened. When she stopped and I looked at her and repeated "I love you" once again, immediately her body language changed. She took a deep breath, her shoulders slumped and she hung her head like a sorrowful child. It was as if all the fight—all the anger and defensiveness—suddenly drained completely out of her. I repeated those same three little words one more time and as I did, she looked up at me with a *completely* changed countenance.

After this breakthrough, we had the most amazing conversation. Not only did she hear me (and actually apologized for what she had done) but I was able to hear her heart and understand her motives in a way I never had before. We both took a few steps that evening toward building a bridge over the large gulf that had separated us.

Everything wasn't resolved that night, but love did win the day. I would not have been able to authentically love her if I had not first allowed his love to change my heart toward her. And his love could never have changed my heart toward her if

I didn't first personally *know* his love. On my own, I simply don't have that much love in me. But I do have his Spirit in me — and he is Love.

Love *is* the key to change. Love is the greatest commandment. Love is the antidote to the fear that hinders change — *"perfect love casts out fear"* (1 John 4:18). Love endures forever. It really does all comes down to love. In the words of that simple, but beautiful hymn by Peter Scholtes:

> *We are one in the Spirit; we are one in the Lord*
>
> *We are one in the Spirit; we are one in the Lord*
>
> *And we know that all unity will one day be restored*
>
> *And they'll know we are Christians by our love,*
>
> *by our love; they will know we are Christians by our love*

Yes, one day they *will* know we are Christians by our love. But we can't give away what we don't have. The world will know his love when we *truly* know it for ourselves.

.

CHAPTER 3

That We May Know Him

*W*hat is the meaning of life? Why am I here? What is my purpose? These are the lofty questions that have kept philosophers, poets, and scientists alike awake at night since the beginning of time. There is an innate longing in the human heart for significance and purpose. We all want our lives to count for something.

Jesus made the answer to this seemingly complex question very simple: *"This is eternal life, that they may know you the only true God"* (John 17:3). The purpose of our lives—here and throughout eternity—is to know him. We were created for fellowship with our Creator. If we miss this one thing, we miss the very foundation of our existence.

People of "One Thing"

Many through the ages *have* grasped this fundamental truth and have come to understand the power of a laser-like focus on "one thing." In Psalm 27:4, David's heart cries out: *"One thing I ask of the LORD, this is what I seek: that I may dwell in the house of the LORD all the days of my life, to gaze upon the beauty of the LORD and seek him in his temple."* David so longed to know God that he made this pursuit the greatest priority and passion of his life. David's devotion did not go unnoticed by God. Despite his many failures and flaws, David will forever be remembered as the man after God's own heart.

Mary of Bethany was another pilgrim whose radical devotion to Jesus was commended by the Lord himself. The story of Mary and her sister Martha (found in Luke 10:38-42) has been told many times and in many ways. Most often, Martha is described as the strong-willed but faithful servant who let her priorities get a bit out of order. Mary, on the other hand, is depicted as the softer, gentler spirit who chose to sit meekly at the feet of the Master instead of helping her sister. I'm not sure this description is entirely accurate.

Martha did what was typical and expected in her culture — she busied herself tending to her guests' needs. But Mary exhibited an extremely bold disregard for the protocol of the day. Not only did she leave her sister and ignore her household duties, she actually *joined the men* sitting at the feet of a respected Rabbi. In that culture, her actions would have been considered scandalous! Put in the context of the times, Martha's annoyance with Mary is all the more understandable — and Jesus' defense of Mary's choice all the more remarkable.

Mary tapped into something many of us still miss: *When Jesus is present, stop what you are doing and listen.* Martha became worried and distracted by the work at hand and as a result missed the opportunity to lean in and hear the heartbeat of the One she was created to know. Jesus confirmed that only "one thing" was needed and that Mary had chosen that better part. It has always been interesting — and comforting — to me that

Jesus also added, *"and it will not be taken away from her"* (Luke 10:42).

No one can take away the opportunity for us to know the Lord. No one can take us away from his presence. No one can deny us the opportunity to sit at his feet. It is a choice — pure and simple. But it is also a choice that will *always* be tested.

In his letter to the Philippians, Paul wrote: *"One thing I do: Forgetting what is behind and straining toward what is ahead, I press on toward the goal to win the prize for which God has called me heavenward in Christ Jesus"* (Phil. 3:13-14). Paul was confined to a Roman prison when he wrote to the Philippians and his circumstances were probably far more adverse than anything most of us will ever experience. Yet his focus was still on the prize. His eyes were on Jesus. Paul was determined that nothing and no one would keep him from knowing Christ. His mind and heart were set on things above (Col. 3:1-2) and he knew that the call "heavenward" could be fulfilled anywhere and under any circumstances. Paul wasn't going to let anything stand in his way of finishing the race God had laid out for him.

Counting All Things Loss

Philippians 3 is one of my all-time favorite passages of Scripture. I have always "heard" the longing in Paul's heart as he declares in v.10, *"I want to know Christ and the power of his resurrection and the fellowship of sharing in his sufferings."* Paul wanted to know all there was to know about Jesus and he didn't care what it cost:

> *"But whatever was to my profit, I now consider loss for the sake of Christ. What is more, I consider everything a loss compared to the surpassing greatness of knowing Christ Jesus, my Lord, for whose sake I have lost all things. I consider them rubbish that I may gain Christ."* **–Phil. 3:7-9**

Paul chose knowing Christ above all the world had to offer — and his life demonstrated the reality of that choice. Like so many things, it is much easier to "say" we want to know Jesus at any cost than it is to actually walk it out. Our resolve will always be tested. Without the proving of our faith, it is easy to develop romanticized notions about what it may look like to "give our all" for the sake of knowing the Lord.

In the previous chapter I mentioned a move I made about fifteen years ago. That move was, at the time, the single biggest leap of faith I had ever made. At that time in my life there were several areas where I felt stuck and also a specific personal situation that needed to be addressed with significant change. I had just gone through a period of deep healing in my own heart and I had been sensing that God was bringing me into a new season. I was excited and thought it would be a time when I would see breakthrough in the areas I had been praying about and waiting on for some time. When a door appeared to open for me to move to an entirely new area, it seemed to line up perfectly with the things the Lord had been speaking to me.

There was a huge amount of risk involved, including leaving my job, church family, and friends among other things, but I was excited for something new and I was up for the challenge. I thought I was quite brave and even felt a bit like Abraham, setting out on an adventure with God into new and unknown territory. But the "adventure" didn't work out the way I thought it was going to work out. I jumped in with both feet and ran forward at full speed ... and about six months later I hit the wall with an enormous thud.

I thought (at the time) I had sacrificed so much. I left everything familiar to follow the Lord where I believed he was leading me. When things kept getting worse instead of better, I was incredibly discouraged and disappointed. I felt confused and utterly defeated. On one particular day, things came to a head. I was absolutely desperate for some kind direction or encouragement, so I grabbed my Bible and randomly flipped it open. I just "happened" to open to Philippians 3. There was that passage again: *"More than that, I count all things to be loss in view of the surpassing value of knowing Christ Jesus my Lord, for whom I have suffered the loss of all things, and count them but rubbish in order that I may gain Christ"* (Phil 3:8, NASB).

I had a box around the entire verse. I had it highlighted. I had it underlined. As if that were not enough, I had even marked the text with a nifty little star. I was serious about it— or so I thought.

Before I could even react, the Lord called me on it:

Really? Do you really want to know me? Do you really count all things loss? Really?

It was *not* what I wanted to hear. I wish I could say my heart immediately received his words and answered with a resounding "Yes!" but that isn't what happened. I was mad. I shoved my Bible aside and continued on with my pity party which, of course, did absolutely nothing to resolve the dilemma I was facing. I felt as though I had put all my eggs in one basket, then tripped and broke them all. I didn't know how God could have let that happen and I was not terribly happy with him.

I didn't have any idea what to do, but somehow I got through the rest of the day. That night as I got ready for bed I had an unshakeable realization—I couldn't go on without more of him. I had already come too far. I couldn't go back; there was absolutely nothing to go back to. I got down on my knees and said the only thing that came to mind, "Lord, to whom shall I go? You alone have the words of eternal life" (John 6:68

paraphrased). I wasn't too keen on his plan at the moment, but I knew I didn't have a better one. And I knew I needed him.

I slept amazingly well that night. When I woke up the next morning, the presence of the Lord immediately surrounded me. Despite the confusion and unbelief of the previous day — not to mention my lousy attitude — Jesus greeted me with tenderness and mercy. Almost as soon as I opened my eyes, it was as if he leaned over and playfully whispered in my ear: *Do you still want to know me?* This time I didn't hesitate. I *knew* the answer was "Yes" in a way that was deeper and far more real than it had ever been in the past.

It wasn't an easy season, but I learned so much. I learned things about myself and, more importantly, I learned about his faithfulness. I came to know him better. When I look back now and recall how tender and gentle he was with me during this season as he helped me through the various circumstances I was facing, it still makes me weep. My heart was a bit fragile during this time and he knew it. He kept telling me he didn't mind proving his faithfulness to me. And he did — over and over again. It is important to note that he still didn't do anything close to what I thought he was going to do, but he did do something better — he gave me more of himself.

I learned an important principle during this season that I have never forgotten: Intimacy with Jesus is never, *ever*, based on performance or circumstances. The world judges based on outward appearances, but God *always* looks on the heart. When I reflect on my relationship with the Lord and what it is that has enabled me to keep moving forward through times of disappointment and difficulty — to keep pressing on, as Paul would say — it is in learning to run *to* him in my pain, brokenness, and failures, rather than *away* from him in shame, confusion, or anger. I've learned to run to him, because I've come to know and trust his heart.

I have taken several other significant leaps of faith since that first one. Quite honestly, most of them have not worked out quite as I had hoped or expected. There have been different blessings and different challenges each time, but I have *always* come out knowing more of his heart. And *that* is worth any price.

Learning His Ways

Like any other relationship, our relationship with the Lord should grow and mature over time. The greater the priority we place on the relationship the more it thrives and grows (note I said on the "relationship" and *not* on religious activity). I have met believers who spend their entire lives in the infancy stages of faith, primarily because they don't want to change or learn — *they're not teachable.* On the other hand, I've met those with incredibly open and hungry hearts who have quickly and whole-heartedly yielded themselves to Jesus and, as a result, have matured rapidly in the greenhouse environment of his presence.

My own relationship with Jesus has changed significantly through the years. I used to be convinced there was a right and wrong answer for everything. And, of course, I *only* wanted the right answers! I only wanted God's will in every area of my life. I only wanted to do what pleased him most. Despite the absolute sincerity of my heart in this endeavor, I fell short far more often than I care to admit. In hindsight, it is painfully obvious that I missed the mark more than a time or two along the way. I didn't understand why the Lord didn't make it easier to get things right, when clearly that was my desire. I finally realized there isn't always a right answer — only a right way. That way is walking in the faithfulness of daily intimate communion with him.

It surprised me greatly when I figured out that sometimes God didn't even care whether or not I got the "right" answer. There were times making the right choice was critical, to be sure, but he was more concerned about nudging me forward into a living, breathing, and growing *relationship* with him.

In the initial stages of my journey with Jesus, it seemed there usually *was* a right answer, or at least I convinced myself there was! And, in truth, I absolutely did need to lay a foundation of obedience to his Word and to his authority in my life. I long ago accepted the fact that only one of us gets to be God in this relationship and it isn't me! He *is* Lord of my life and when I *know* he is asking me to do something—I do it. Period.

However, since that foundation has been laid, he allows me great liberty. When this shift first started taking place it was a bit puzzling to me. As was my habit, I would seek the Lord whenever I had a decision to make. But for the longest time instead of an answer when I asked him about something, over and over again I would hear: *"What do you think?"* -or- *"What do you want to do?"* It was a completely new paradigm for me. I didn't like it! I wanted him to *tell* me what was best.

This had been going on for some time when I asked Jesus about yet another decision to be made on a particular day. This time I really wanted an answer, so when I asked him I added, "And *please* don't say, 'What do *you* think?'"

But he didn't say anything at all.

A bit later, I tried again. I reasoned with the Lord that this was important. The issue in question was whether or not to give up the one day of the week I had set aside to rest in his presence in order to drive out to another city to connect with a pastor from another country. A mutual friend had felt this would be a significant and important ministry connection. I had no problem going if it was the right thing to do, but I didn't want to give up my day off if it really wasn't a big deal. I really wanted to know what Jesus thought—but he was silent.

Finally, toward the end of the day—at the point I would need to be making arrangements if I was going to go—I tried another tactic. Ever tried to twist God's arm in something? Ask me how well it worked! But I tried anyway.

"C'mon Lord, please! When you love someone, sometimes you just want to *know* you're doing what pleases them. I really just want to *know* what you want me to do. Help! Please?"

I was about to give up on an answer and just make plans to go, when he had mercy on me and began to answer my poor, pitiful plea. Somehow I sensed he was about to ask me a question. I wanted answers—not questions—so I cut him off at the start and said, "And please *don't* ask me what I think!"

Thankfully, I didn't deter him. It seems he was finally in the mood to talk.

I wasn't going to ask "What do you think?" I was going to ask, "Why do you think I always ask you what you think?"

"Well, it certainly isn't because you need to know. Clearly, you already know exactly what I think all the time!"

He graciously ignored my sarcasm and continued.

Maybe it's because I want you to know how much you already know what I think.

Hmm … I can't say I ever thought of that. He went on.

You know, you're right. When you love someone it's great to ask them what they want and do that very thing. But do you know what's even better?

He didn't wait for me to respond.

What's better is when you know someone so well you don't have to ask – you just do what pleases them.

Oh …

As soon as he spoke those words, I knew *exactly* what to do. It seemed so incredibly obvious that I couldn't remember why I had been so confused. I would stay home to rest and hang out with him, because I *knew* that would please him. Once this decision had been quickly reached, I heard simple, sweet words that I have come to treasure in my heart each and every time he has spoken them to me:

Yes beloved, you've chosen the better part.

He went on to remind me that if the meeting had been significant to his timing and purposes, he could have arranged for it to fit easily into my schedule. Or I would have had a deep compelling to go, rather than indifference and confusion. It was another life lesson in simply learning to walk with him and allowing him to teach me *his* ways.

"If you are pleased with me, teach me your ways so I may know you and continue to find favor with you" (Ex.33:13). This has always been one of my most frequent prayers. More than anything, I want to *know* him. David – the man after God's heart – prayed similar prayers on more than one occasion (see Ps.27 and Ps. 86). Mary of Bethany boldly defied tradition because she *had* to be close to Jesus. This same Mary was the only one in tune enough with his heart that she understood he was going to the cross (see Mark 14:8). Paul so longed to know Jesus that he was willing to suffer the loss of absolutely everything else to gain this "one thing." These, and others throughout history, heard the heartbeat of heaven and discovered the very meaning of life itself: *That we may know him.*

May we, too, be a people of "one thing." A people who seek to know his ways. A people who, like the Apostle John "the disciple Jesus loved," lean upon his chest to hear his heartbeat. And as we come to know his heart, may we join him in *his* heart's desire for one Church, one body—and one bride.

CHAPTER 4

The Need for Endurance

I must have been quite the sight, standing indecisively in the middle of a busy parking lot having a conversation with my "invisible" Friend.

For some time the Lord had been speaking to me about the importance of exhibiting his character in small things. Very small things. Like cleaning up after others in the office without grumbling. Or picking up trash that someone else carelessly dropped. Or always returning my shopping cart.

It was the shopping cart that got me that day. It had been a long day and I was tired. The store was crowded and everything took too long. Eventually I got what I needed and left. I walked what seemed like two blocks to get back to my car and after I unloaded my purchases I looked for the nearest shopping cart stall. There wasn't one nearby, but there *were* shopping carts strewn all over the parking lot. I saw several bunched together not terribly far from where I was. I reasoned that it wouldn't hurt — just this once — to drop my cart off with several others instead of taking it all the way back where it belonged. After all, someone was going to have to come get all those other carts anyway. Right?

It made sense to me, so that was my plan. I got about halfway back to my car when I felt the familiar nudge of the Holy Spirit. I tried to tell myself I was imagining it—seriously, would God really care about a shopping cart that didn't "quite" get put back where it belonged? I walked another few steps toward my car but the impression that I needed to turn around got stronger and stronger with each step.

That's when I stopped and just stood there. I was thinking about how foolish I must look. By this time I was nearly all the way back to my car. I thought it would look pretty ridiculous (as if anyone was watching) to turn back, pick up my shopping cart where I left it, take one little shopping cart all the way to the front when there were so many others scattered all about, and then walk back again. That's what *I* thought. But the Lord had another opinion. His words couldn't have been any clearer:

Finish the job.

The Cost of Discipleship

Obviously those three little words carried a depth of meaning far beyond returning a shopping cart (which I did do, by the way). Returning the cart really wasn't that big a deal, but the principle it represented *was*: We need to be committed to finishing what we start. Specifically, we need to be committed to finishing what *he has called us to do* — especially when it is much easier not to do so.

During his earthly ministry, Jesus had some pretty straightforward and difficult things to say about the cost of being his disciple and "finishing the job":

"Suppose one of you wants to build a tower. Will he not first sit down and estimate the cost to see if he has enough money to complete it? For if he lays the foundation and is not able to finish it, everyone who sees it will ridicule him, saying, 'This fellow began to build and was not able to finish.'

"Or suppose a king is about to go to war against another king. Will he not first sit down and consider whether he is able with ten thousand men to oppose the one coming against him with twenty thousand? If he is not able, he will send a delegation while the other is still a long way off and will ask for terms of peace. In the same way, any of you who does not give up everything he has cannot be my disciple." –**Luke 14:28-33**

Being a true disciple of Christ is costly. Expecting it to be otherwise will quickly lead to disillusionment and disappointment. Jesus made this clear over and over again. Jesus promised us abundant life, but he *never* indicated that such a life would be free from pain and adversity. In fact, he said quite the opposite: *"In this world you will have trouble. But take heart! I have overcome the world"* (John 16:33). He knows we are living in a fallen world filled with challenges. But he also knows that isn't the end of the story because he has given us the grace to both persevere *and* overcome.

We persevere by keeping our eyes on the prize—by keeping the end in mind. (Remember, you can't separate the end from the beginning!) Jesus didn't promise our journey on this side would be easy, but he did promise it would be worthwhile. When Peter asked the Lord what their reward would be for having left all to follow him, Jesus made this amazing statement: *"And everyone who has left houses or brothers or sisters or father or mother or children or fields for my sake will* receive a hundred times as much and will inherit eternal life" (Matt.19:29). This same conversation is recorded again in Mark 10:29, where Mark clarifies the promise is applicable *to the present time* (along with "persecutions" which he so helpfully includes!), as well as in the age to come. There is a reward here and now—and an even greater reward for all of eternity—for those who *"run in such a way as to get the prize"* (1 Cor.9:24). As Paul so eloquently put it: *"I consider that our present sufferings are not worth comparing with the glory that will be revealed in us"* (Romans 8:18). Whatever price we pay in this life for the sake of Christ, we can rest assured—it *will* be worth it!

Jesus had his eyes on the prize in John 17 when he said, *"I have glorified You on the earth. I have finished the work which You have given Me to do. And now, O Father, glorify Me together with Yourself, with the glory which I had with You before the world was"* (John 17:4-5 NKJV). Jesus knew he was glorifying the Father by *finishing* the job he had been given to do. He would be returning to the Father to share his glory once again—*after* he made a way for us to join him. Though Jesus was almost finished with his earthly assignment, the cross was still ahead. He was purposefully setting his gaze on *"the joy set before him"* (Heb. 12:2) so he would have the strength to finish the race.

Those Who Have Endured

There are certain words we're not terribly fond of in Christian circles. Words like "patience" "perseverance" and "endurance." We live in a world of microwaves and fast food— we want it our way and we want it now. But instant gratification doesn't usually translate well into matters of faith. Maybe things consistently work out quickly for some people— if you're one of them, God bless you!—but most of us need to make peace with the concept of endurance.

The Bible is filled with stories of those who had to learn to endure. Moses tried to deliver the children of Israel out of the hand of Pharaoh on his own with disastrous results. After that he spent forty years on the back side of the desert learning patience. When God did call Moses and sent him back to Pharaoh, Moses was no longer confident in his own abilities, *but he learned to be confident in God's*. David was just a kid when he was anointed as king of Israel, but it was years and years before he took the throne. He spent many of the years in between developing character and perseverance while being hunted down by his crazed and jealous predecessor, Saul.

Perhaps one of the best known stories of endurance is that of Abraham. Abraham was seventy-five years old when God called him out of Haran and promised to make him the father of many nations; he was the ripe old age of a hundred when Isaac was finally born. Since Abraham was already so old when the promise came, I'm sure he thought he had waited long enough and that God would begin fulfilling his word right away. *But he waited another 25 years.* His faith is recorded in the book of Romans this way:

> *Against all hope, Abraham in hope believed and so became the father of many nations, just as it had been said to him, "So shall your offspring be." Without weakening in his faith, he faced the fact that his body was as good as dead — since he was about a hundred years old — and that Sarah's womb was also dead. Yet he did not waver through unbelief regarding the promise of God, but was strengthened in his faith and gave glory to God, being fully persuaded that God had power to do what he had promised.* **–Romans 4:18-21**

God *did* what he promised. That's the point of each of these stories. There was much waiting and many twists and turns on each journey, but ultimately *God did what he promised.* None of them waited perfectly—they had times of doubt and made many mistakes along the way—but God still did what he promised. Moses did deliver the children of Israel from the hand of Pharaoh. David did become king of Israel. And Abraham became the father of many nations.

In fact, God not only fulfilled his promises in each of these men's lives—*he did more.* Moses wasn't just a deliverer—he *saw* the glory of God and spoke to him face-to-face as a friend. David not only ruled over Israel in his lifetime, but was assured that One from his lineage would rule from that same throne—*forever.* And Abraham didn't just have a son—he gave us a glimpse of *the* Son in the clearest foretaste of the great redemption to come when he faithfully offered his promised son back to the Lord as a sacrifice, only to have "God himself provide the lamb" (see Gen.22).

Waiting with Gratitude

Almost all of us have unfulfilled promises in our lives. We all wait for something. We all have those areas where we are invited to press in and press on. They are usually different from one person to the next. Some things have come easily in my life that may require a great deal of perseverance in yours. On the other hand, I have waited for things that others have received quickly and with little effort.

It is often our very human nature to focus on what we do not have and on what we are waiting for, rather than on what we *do* have and on what God has already done. However, it is in purposing to do the opposite—focusing on what God *has* done and what he is doing, rather than on what he *hasn't* done—that cultivates the attitude of gratitude that not only helps us endure, but also positions us for breakthrough.

Perspective brings gratitude—and gratitude brings perspective. When my heart is grateful, I'm able to genuinely rejoice with those who have (sometimes quickly) received a breakthrough for which I have waited years but have yet to receive. On the flip side, it also enables me to be more sensitive to those who are struggling to lay hold of things that have come more easily for me. It is a true test of our character when someone offers "victory lessons" in an area of struggle when you know that person has *not* had the same degree of struggle. It's not usually helpful when someone suggests you "just" do such and such, when you have already been doing those things—and often more—for years, or even decades, seemingly to no avail.

God alone sees the whole picture in each of our lives. We would do well to remember that when tempted to offer unsolicited advice others. We *never* have the full story. It is always a good idea to check in with the Holy Spirit before carelessly dispensing the platitudes and band-aid solutions that make waiting even more difficult. Although most of the time we *do* genuinely want to support and encourage each other, we simply don't have the capacity to walk a mile in someone else's shoes. I have a friend, Sheri, who has struggled with severe Type I Diabetes most of her life. She has had many sincere brothers and sisters through the years come alongside who have *believed* for her healing. Each one has meant well, but as she humorously says, "I wore them all out!"

Sheri has a great attitude and I know she will see complete healing, but in the meantime I know how she feels. When something takes a particularly long time you start to feel bad for the people praying for you and want something to happen for their sakes! We all love the "big" testimony. We love the big stories of God actually doing the things we've hoped and prayed he would do. But I have learned that is only one type of testimony — there is another (often more costly) type of testimony that is very precious in the eyes of the Lord.

A Testimony of Perseverance — and Hope

For about five years I served with a large global missions organization. Twice a year we would have candidates for field service come into our office for training. As part of their training the candidates learned to publicly give their testimony. One day in chapel, I was listening to the testimony of a remarkable young woman. She was recounting the amazing things God had done in her life in a very short period of time. Many of those blessings were the very same things I had been praying about for many years without any sign of breakthrough or movement. I was so excited for her — God used those things to reveal more of himself to her and she was literally glowing with joy and gratitude — but I also had a familiar ache in my own heart where those desires remained unfulfilled. I told the Lord I was so happy for her, but I longed for a similar testimony of breakthrough in my own life. Jesus told me I *did* have a testimony — I had a testimony of perseverance.

It is indeed very precious to the Lord when we continue to believe though we have not yet seen. This has been a familiar theme in my life for many years, and in many, many areas. There is a tension between the "now" and the "not yet." We need to learn to walk in joy and gratitude for all we have here and now, while at the same time exercising "bull dog" faith that *won't let go* of specific promises that have not yet been fulfilled. We need to enjoy the journey — *daily* — but we also need to keep the goal in sight. It is so easy to focus on only one or the other, and so very difficult to walk in the tension between the two.

Before the start of every New Year, I seek the Lord for a Scripture for the coming year. What I start out believing that year's word means, and what it actually ends up meaning are often two very different things. The last several years have been no exception. A few years ago, the Lord gave me Proverbs 13:12, *"Hope deferred makes the heart sick, but when the desire comes, it is a tree of life"* (NKJV). Of course, my emphasis—and hope—was on the "when the desire comes" part of the verse. But that was not to be the case (yet). Instead the year brought what seemed to be the death of a longstanding dream in the closure of a ministry I had hoped to spend my life serving. Definitely *not* what I had in mind!

The following year my verse (also from the NKJV) was Psalm 27:13, *"I would have lost heart unless I believed I would see the goodness of the Lord in the land of the living."* While this was a year of transition that brought many positive changes, it was also a year in which I dangled closer to that dangerous precipice called "losing heart" than I ever had before. Since I no longer felt expectant in several areas, I was fearful that I was beginning to settle into a degree of complacency that would ultimately make me willing to settle for less than *all* Jesus had promised.

As I approached the beginning of another new year, once again, I was hearing many amazing testimonies from people. While they encouraged and strengthened me, again I found myself wondering when—*or if*—I would have a "big" testimony of my own. And, once again, the Lord challenged my perspective and reminded me there was more than one kind of testimony. He asked me about my "reality in him" over the past year. Had it increased? I was able to honestly answer that I had gained more revelation and insight into his ways during that particular year than I had in the past ten combined. He responded very simply: *Then it was a very good year.*

It *was* a good year. Jesus went on to draw my attention back to Proverbs 13:12 and showed me that while I had experienced very real heartsickness due to unfulfilled desires, the second part of the verse spoke about *when* the desire comes — not *if* — *when*. It was a promise. Then he reminded me of the past year's verse: *I would have lost heart unless I believed I would see the goodness of the Lord in the land of the living.* He leaned over and gently whispered in my ear: *You didn't lose heart.* Though I didn't always feel steadfast and I had faced circumstances that could very easily have led to giving up in several areas, I chose instead to believe him (and not my feelings) and hold on to hope. He then confirmed my verse for the coming year: *I have come that they may have life; and have it more abundantly* (John 10:10 NKJV).

It was then that I noticed the theme in each of these verses: Life! Abundant life and *living* hope. What a testimony it is to his faithfulness when we come to trust in his love and goodness in such a way that we not only still believe after many losses and disappointments, but we actually believe more! James 1:12 says: *"Blessed is the man who perseveres under trial because when he has stood the test, he will receive the crown of life that God has promised to those who love him."* As the writer of Hebrews puts it: *"Do not cast away your confidence which has great reward. For you have need of endurance, so that after you have done the will of God you will receive the promise"* (Heb.10:35-36 NKJV).

You will receive the promise! I will receive the promise! But we have need of endurance. God will do his part — but we must continue to do ours. We do our part by *not* casting away our confidence *in him*. I know he *will* be faithful and I know I *will* see the goodness of the Lord in the land of the living. In fact, I see more and more of his goodness each and every day I set my gaze on him.

Although I eagerly await the day his promises will come to pass (and they will), far more compelling than seeing the reality of God's promises fulfilled, is the promise of seeing *him*. I believe one of the most profound verses in all of Scripture on the concept of endurance is a very simple one: "*He* (Moses) *endured as seeing him who is invisible*" (Heb. 11:27). As amazing as the promises are, the promises are not the reward—*Jesus is the reward.* Above anything and everything else, the one thing that propels me to endure is the knowledge that I will see his face. I will stand before him and I will give an account for my life. I desire to live my life with a keen daily awareness of that moment. When I look into his eyes on that day, I desperately want to be able to say: "I have finished the work you have given *me* to do." Because only then will I hear *him* say the words my heart is so longing to hear:

Well done good and faithful servant! ... Come and share your master's happiness! –**Matt. 25:23**

II. "REVEALING THE FATHER"

Hearts Aligned with His

*"I have revealed you to those you have given me out of the world." –***John 17:6**

$\mathcal{A}$fter Jesus had prayed for himself, he turned his attention to praying for his disciples—those in his inner circle who had journeyed with him for the past three years. They were soon to be left in the world as his representatives. Jesus had revealed the heart and character of the Father to them because he knew it was the security of knowing *who they were* and *who they belonged to* that would prepare and equip them for the next stage of their journey.

Lord, align our hearts with your heart and reveal your ways to us. Sanctify us in the truth. As you send us out into the world, let us rightly reflect the beauty of your nature to those around us.

CHAPTER 5

Jesus = Perfect Theology

We gathered with our large study Bibles, our concordances, Bible dictionaries and any other resource we thought would be helpful for the subject at hand. I had been invited by a friend to participate in a discussion with some friends who had become advocates of doctrine that was different from what we adhered to at the time. The subject, essentially, was Arminianism vs. Calvinism. Did the emphasis in our salvation lie on man's freewill to choose, or in God's sovereign election?

The conversation went on for hours and was heated at times. At a certain point we concluded the discussion and went our separate ways. Neither side had been swayed by the other. No greater understanding had been reached.

I went home that night and felt sick to my stomach. I had an enormous appetite for God's Word, but the world of apologetics was new to me. It was an important focus of the church I attended at the time and I knew I was supposed to know what I believed and why I believed it, but I *didn't* see the point of the discussion we just had. All we had accomplished was to further divide and alienate ourselves from each other. I knew that wasn't what God wanted and it broke my heart.

The great irony of that evening is that I had to step back and think long and hard to remember which side of the debate I had been on! It simply wasn't—and still isn't—a point worth arguing. I have since learned a very important lesson when it comes to issues of theology and doctrine: Choose your battles very carefully. That is not to say we should avoid all "spirited" discussions that might lead to conflict or disagreement—we *must* learn to think for ourselves and stand on our convictions—but when our opinions differ, there has to be a point where we agree to disagree agreeably. Most issues simply aren't important enough to risk losing a brother or sister over.

I owe a tremendous debt to the church that gave me a solid foundation of biblical understanding, but somewhere along the way I began to pick up something that wasn't quite so helpful: An unreasonable fear of being wrong or falling into error. I say "unreasonable" because there is a healthy place of "examining yourself to see whether you are in the faith" (2 Cor. 13:5 paraphrased). We do need to keep bringing our hearts before the Lord. We need to stay connected and accountable to each other. And, especially, we need to keep our hearts teachable. But things can go far beyond healthy in a hurry when we start to become suspicious of anyone or anything that doesn't line up with our current, very limited, understanding.

Thankfully, I never went too far down this path, but with the benefit of hindsight I can see areas where I was much more deeply steeped in religious tradition than I ever realized. I still find its tentacles wrapped around areas of my faith from time to time. But I love Jesus more than I love being right. And because I do, my ongoing longing for a true revelation of his heart has protected me from falling too deeply into the trap of religious intellectualism.

The enemy of our souls will do just about anything to distract us from a deeper revelation of the heart of God. The trap of religion is one of hell's most favored ploys. The work of religion feels so spiritual and seems so right. If you were to delve beneath the surface, you would find a vast number of sincere believers are more committed to their favorite biblical principles than they are to seeking — and *yielding* to — the very presence of God. The Holy Spirit is unpredictable and unpredictability is uncomfortable. We want to know what is going to happen and our desire for control moves us from the unpredictable reality of God's presence to the more controlled environment of biblical precepts and principles (otherwise know as "the law"). Control is rooted in fear — and fear hinders both love and life.

Far too often we behave as though we believe more in the devil's power to deceive than we do in God's power to protect and preserve. But the Apostle John exhorts: *"As for you, the anointing you received from him remains in you, and you do not need anyone to teach you. But as his anointing teaches you about all things and as that anointing is real, not counterfeit — just as it has taught you, remain in him"* (1 John 2:27). John is writing about our protection from those who would lead us astray. Our protection isn't found primarily in correct theology, it is found in the reality of Christ himself living in us!

An Answer for the Hope We Have

Does this mean we give up the responsibility to *"always be prepared to give an answer for the hope that you have"* (1 Peter 3:15)? The Greek word translated "give an answer" is "apologia" — which is why we use the word "apologetics" to describe the practice of defending our faith. I've often heard this verse stated as evidence of our responsibility to engage in a defense of our doctrine and beliefs. However, that is not the true emphasis of the passage.

The Lord gave me a little private teaching on this verse some time ago. I was one of the teachers for a women's Bible study at a large church. I was preparing a message and the subject matter was one there had been considerable distorted discussion over in the secular media of late. Instead of focusing on seeking the Lord for what he wanted to communicate to the ladies of the Bible study, I became distracted by all the nonsense that was floating around "out there." Somehow I became convinced that I must have an answer for all the opposing views that were being propagated. Never mind that no one in the Bible study was likely to share such views, I had to have an answer!

I'd spent about an hour on a diligent quest for answers to unasked questions from invisible critics, when the Lord must have decided I'd wasted just about enough time. He interrupted my little research project by asking me what I was doing. I pay special attention whenever Jesus asks me this particular question — when he does, it is usually because I'm not doing what I ought to be doing!

I told him I needed to give an answer for these things. Surely he understood since it was *his* Word that directed me to do so. He kindly suggested I actually read the passage in 1 Peter. This is what the *entire* verse says: *"But in your hearts, always set apart Christ as Lord. Always be ready to give an answer for the hope that you have. But do this with gentleness and respect"* (1 Pet. 3:15). The first thing my eyes were drawn to was the phrase "give an answer for the hope that you have." We are to simply communicate *why we have hope*. Really, it is an invitation to share the reality of *"Christ in me, the hope of glory!"* It is an exhortation to share our personal testimony of hope in Christ —

not an exhortation to give a systematic defense of our personal understanding of Christian doctrine and ideology.

The Holy Spirit went on to remind me that the verse begins with the admonition to "set apart Christ as Lord" in *our hearts,* and ends with the reminder to do all with "gentleness and respect." The verse isn't about defending our faith, it is about thoughtfully and lovingly sharing our hope in Jesus (even under persecution within the context of the entire passage). How this differs from the application I have most often heard of this verse! When I allow Jesus to reign as Lord in my heart, my heart and character become more closely aligned with his own. He is the *God of hope.* He desires that others see hope alive in my life ... so they can have hope too.

In our often misguided zeal to defend our faith and values, the Church has become known more for what she stands *against* than what she stands *for.* Maybe if we really stood for the things Jesus stood for—if we stood for love; if we stood for life; if we stood for the poor and the oppressed; if we stood for the brokenhearted and the lonely; if we stood for redemption and restoration; if we stood for forgiveness and mercy that triumphs over judgment; if we stood for healing and hope; if we stood for freedom—the world would see more of him. And yes, we must also stand for truth, but the truth isn't merely a set of rules and precepts. It also isn't a list of dos and don'ts. The Truth is a Person—and his name is Jesus. He alone is the perfect representation of both the Word *and* the Spirit.

The Spirit Gives Life

Bill Johnson of Bethel Church in Redding, CA, has often been quoted as saying. "Jesus Christ is perfect theology." Issues are complex, but our theology doesn't need to be. Jesus himself said, *"Anyone who has seen me has seen the Father"* (John 14:8). If you want to know God's heart in a matter, look to Jesus. He is *the* Truth.

I will forever be grateful for the priceless gift of God's Word. I *love* the written Word of God and have joyfully spent countless hours mining its treasures. *But without the presence of the Holy Spirit breathing life upon its pages, the Bible alone will never lead to life.* We are so amazingly blessed to live in an age where our bookshelves can be lined with various versions of the Bible, but we would do well to remember that privilege has only been available to us in recent years. Yet God himself has never changed and he communicated with man long before we had access to beautiful leather-bound books with gold gilded pages. The Bible does not *contain* God, but it most certainly does *reveal* him. We are invited into relationship with a Person, *not* a book—no matter how precious and essential that book may be.

It is so vitally important to recognize and be led by the *presence* of God, and not the *precepts* of God alone. In many, many situations, there is Scripture on both sides of an issue. When this is the case, we need to seek the specific counsel of the Holy Spirit to reveal God's heart in the matter. There was a reason God required the Israelites to "inquire of the Lord" before they went into battle. The strategy was different each and every time. They couldn't rely solely on the principles of the last victory; they had to draw near to God to listen and obey in each specific situation. Even Jesus never healed anyone the same way twice. He only did what he saw the Father doing. Jesus wasn't led by precept or principle alone; he was led by the specific instruction of the Holy Spirit.

I've heard many believers suggest that only in-depth study of the Bible can provide answers for the issues of life. It is absolutely true that *"All Scripture is God breathed and is useful for teaching, rebuking, correcting and training in righteousness"* (2 Tim.

3:16). While the Bible is crucial for "training in righteousness" and learning God's ways, it is the reality of *knowing Jesus* that leads to life. Jesus himself said: *"You diligently study the Scriptures because you think that by them you possess eternal life. These are the Scriptures that testify about me, yet you refuse to come to me to have life"* (John 5:39-40). We still need to come to him. Focusing on precepts alone — apart from the reality of his presence — always leads to death. *"For the letter kills, but the Spirit gives life"* (2 Cor. 3:6).

One of the reasons Jesus was such a controversial and offensive figure to the religious leaders of the day is because he did not apply the Scriptures the same way they did. Jesus "did not come to abolish the law or the Prophets, but to fulfill them" (Matt. 5:17 paraphrased). His focus was on revealing and fulfilling the *true* intent of the law. The Pharisees and other religious leaders took pride in keeping *the letter* of the law — to the point that their traditions and doctrine became far more important than seeking the heart of God. Jesus pointed out their hypocrisy by quoting the prophet Isaiah, *"These people honor me with their lips, but their hearts are far from me. They worship me in vain; their teachings are but rules taught by men"* (Matt. 15:8-9).

Having additional Scripture (the New Testament) and professed faith in Jesus does *not* make us immune from falling into the same trap. *"Knowledge puffs up; but love builds up"* (1 Cor. 8:1). It is only an open teachable spirit — and the power and presence of the Holy Spirit — that keeps our love and faith alive. Long before the Bible existed, in the very beginning, the Spirit of God hovered over the formless void of the earth and spoke life into existence. It was the Spirit of God himself that breathed life into Adam's nostrils. It will always be the Spirit that gives life.

A Higher Vision

As a writer, I am keenly aware of the limitations of the written word. No matter how carefully I choose my words there is always the possibility of misunderstanding. The written word alone cannot possibly express all that is in my heart, nor can it fully reveal my personality, character, and motives. It's a start, but there are many things that are still open to conjecture and interpretation. However, the possibility for misunderstanding decreases substantially for those *who know me personally.* When friends read things I've written they often say, "I could totally hear you saying that!" They know what my tone of voice would be. They know the expression I would have on my face. As a result, they understand the words I write at a level that may be foreign to someone who doesn't know me.

The same is true with the written Word of God. Jesus made the Father accessible and knowable. The more we know him, the more we learn his ways, the better we are able to "hear his tone of voice" and "see his expression" when we read the Bible. When we know his heart, we are less likely to misunderstand his Word.

In the Old Testament, the Lord spoke through the prophet Isaiah and said, "*'My thoughts are not your thoughts, neither are my ways, your ways,' declares the LORD. 'As the heavens are high above the earth, so are my ways higher than your ways and my thoughts than your thoughts.'*" (Isaiah 55:8-9). Yet in the New Testament, Paul says *"But we have the mind of Christ"* (1 Cor. 2:16).

Part of understanding the heart and mind of God requires embracing the mystery of the paradox—the reality that two seemingly contradictory things can be true at the same time (for more on this concept see Chapter 13). God is infinite and we are finite, but the mystery of Christ *in us* allows us to tap into the reality of his infinite wisdom.

Western culture (including church culture) has been greatly molded and influenced by Greek thinking, which is static and linear. Greek thinking says one plus one equals two; 'a' leads to 'b', then 'b' leads to 'c', etc. Hebraic thinking, on the other hand, is dynamic and driven by "block logic" which focuses on blocks of subject matter rather than formal and logical (linear) reasoning. According to scholar Marvin Wilson, truth, to the Hebraic mind, is "not so much an idea to be contemplated as an experience to be lived, a deed to be done." When we contemplate the infinite "mind of Christ" — the mind of the Holy One of Israel — we can be certain that all truth will *not* fall into nice, neat, linear lines of logic.

Once again, it was a personal object lesson that brought this concept from my head to my heart. After much prayer and prophetic encouragement, in early 2007 I expanded and incorporated my ministry and established a small house of prayer as our base of operation. From a lovely little building we called *The Well*, we enjoyed a challenging, but oh so glorious, season of seeking the Lord and proclaiming his heart's desire over individuals, the region we lived in, and the nations of the earth. After much wrestling with the Lord, I even gave up a wonderful position with a large Christian retreat and conference center to focus full-time on this little ministry. However, just over a year and a half later, financial circumstances caused us to close the doors and forced me to take a job in an arena to which I had hoped to never to return.

For several months prior to closing our doors things had not looked good financially, yet over and over again the Lord's encouragement was "to stand." We did. Then one day there was a tangible shift and his release to move on was just as clear as the previous exhortation to stand had been. Although we knew we needed to let go, it was heartbreaking. It was particularly difficult for me personally, since my life had seemed to be a progression of steps that culminated in the birth of that ministry. In closing it down and finding it necessary to return to work in a "tent-making" occupation, I felt like I was going backwards by at least a good ten years. Needless to say, I didn't understand and wondered where I had gone wrong.

While we still had the prayer room, I sneaked away from church one Sunday morning and met the Lord there. It was another of those encounters difficult to express within the confines of human language, but the Lord made one thing very clear. While I felt like a failure, Jesus didn't see it that way at all. He measures success in terms of faithfulness, as opposed to specific results, and in *his* eyes it had all been a smashing success. He even promised I would one day see the fruit of the prayers we had prayed from that place. I literally *felt* his pleasure over my willingness to make such a personal sacrifice in what I had given up to start the ministry in the first place — and in what I was now giving up to move on.

God's wisdom is higher than ours. The true essence of what he did for me that day was that he invited me up to his throne to view the situation from his perspective. I had been telling Jesus I felt like I was going backwards. His perspective was that it wasn't about going forward *or* backwards — *it was about coming up higher*. From heaven's perspective our journey is not a linear line on which you can only move forward or backwards — it is a sphere of influence that is ever increasing the higher we climb. In my case, one and one didn't equal two, and faithfulness didn't look like the linear line I thought my journey should take. But I *was* within the "sphere" of his will and purposes for my life. Even more, it was clear he was downright joyful about that fact — *and* about my future.

Jesus revealed the Father's heart for me in the midst of my circumstances and *that* is what enabled me to keep moving forward—which was really upward. Theology and right doctrine have not kept my feet secure when the journey has been difficult; it has been the love and acceptance I've found in the face of Jesus that has kept me on the path of life. Because I've seen Jesus, I've seen the Father. And because I've seen from his perspective ...

I press on toward the goal to win the prize for which God has called me heavenward in Christ Jesus. –**Phil 3:14**

.

CHAPTER 6

The Power of His Name

One evening Jesus and his disciples headed out to sea. Before they ever got in the boat, Jesus said "*Let us go to the other side*" (Mark 4:35). It sounded simple enough, of course they were going to the other side, that's why they got in the boat in the first place. But something happened along the way. A furious storm overtook them. The waves broke over the boat and it was nearly filled with water. The disciples were sure they were going to drown. And where was Jesus during the calamity? Asleep on a cushion in the stern of the boat.

The disciples woke him with an accusation, "*Teacher, don't you care if we drown?*" *He got up, rebuked the wind and said to the waves, "Quiet! Be still!" Then the wind died down and it was completely calm* (Mark 4:38-39). Once he had calmed the storm, Jesus had a few questions of his own, "*Why are you so afraid? Do you still have no faith?*" (Mark 4:40).

Tough questions, to be sure, but that isn't what gets me about the story. What gets me is the disciples' reaction after Jesus' question: "*They were terrified and asked each other, 'Who is this? Even the wind and waves obey him!'*" (Mark 4:41).

Who is this? This is the most important question we will ever face in our lives. Who is this One who possesses such authority that even the elements of creation obey him? Who is he — *really*? Knowing the answer changes everything.

Like the disciples, we can walk with Jesus, talk with Jesus, and even have a very genuine ongoing relationship with him without *truly* grasping the reality of who he is. Clearly Jesus' response to the disciple's indicates he felt they should have understood more than they did. Despite that, it has always encouraged me that even though they didn't get it right, *he still helped them.* That fact itself reveals a facet of who he is — he is merciful and he doesn't wait for us to get it right before he steps in to help. I'm so glad!

I don't always get it right, either. I want to. I deeply desire to grow in my knowledge of God — moment by moment, day by day, year by year — but I don't always grasp as much as I would like to, as quickly as I would like to. But despite my weakness — *he still is who he is* — his faithfulness to his character and nature is not dependent upon *my* understanding.

I AM that I AM

In Scripture, there has always been great significance placed on the name of God. Moses was the first person to whom God revealed his name (Exod. 3:13-16). God later told Moses that although Abraham, Isaac and Jacob had known him as "God Almighty," he had not revealed *his name* to them as he had to Moses (Exod. 6:2-3). God revealed himself to Moses as "I AM that I AM." It is so interesting to me that God gave Moses his name *after Moses asked.* I wonder how much more God would entrust himself to *us* if we simply pressed in and asked?

When Jesus prayed for his disciples he said, *"Holy Father, protect them by the power of your name — the name you gave me —*

that they may be one as we are one" (John 17:11). Jesus not only confirms it is the power of God's name that protects us, but it is also his name that binds us together.

In his prayer, Jesus declares that God gave him the *same name*. In this and several other instances, John's gospel gives clear evidence of Jesus as the pre-existent and uncreated One. The very first verse of John's gospel starts out with this amazing reality, *"In the beginning was the Word and the Word was with God and the Word was God. He was with God in the beginning"* (John 1:1-2). A few verses later John conclusively identifies "the Word" as Jesus: *"The Word became flesh and made his dwelling among us"* (John 1:14). In addition, Jesus identified himself with the Father's name in the many key "I Am" statements throughout the book of John:

- I AM the bread of life (John 6:35).
- I AM the light of the world (John 8:12).
- I AM the door (or "the gate" depending on the translation, John 10:7).
- I AM the good shepherd (John 10:11).
- I AM the resurrection and the life (John 11:25).
- I AM the way, the truth and the life (John 14:6).
- I AM the true vine (John 15:1).

Each statement reveals another profound key to God's nature but arguably the most amazing statement Jesus makes about himself occurs in John, chapter 8:

> *Jesus replied ... "Your father Abraham rejoiced at the thought of seeing my day; he saw it and was glad."*

"You are not yet 50 years old," the Jews said to him, *"and you have seen Abraham!"*

"I tell you the truth," Jesus answered, *"Before Abraham was, I am!"* –**John 8:56-58**

Judging by the Jews' reaction (they picked up rocks in an attempt to stone him) there was no doubt in their minds that Jesus was claiming to share the covenant name God had revealed to Moses: The Great I AM. And indeed he is everything we need, everything we hope for, everything we desire—and more!

We could study the nature and character of God for all of eternity and not even begin to scratch the surface of all he is, all he has done, all he is currently doing, and all he *will* do. I have a friend who has ministered several times in the nation of Brazil. After one trip, Ted came back and told of a twenty-four hour place of prayer and worship devoted solely to meditating on and worshiping the names of God. Every hour a different attribute of God is highlighted—one of his names—so that those coming into the prayer room can meditate upon that particular facet of God's nature. Twenty-four hours a day, seven days a week, this goes on, with a different name and attribute of God highlighted each and every hour of each and every day. He described it as one of most awesome places of worship he had ever experienced! This amazing multi-faceted Being is the One to whom *we* belong. *"The name of the Lord is a strong tower; the righteous run into it and are safe!"* (Proverbs 18:10). We are secure in him!

Transformed into His Likeness

As I concentrate on different aspects of God's nature, I have noticed there is a correlation between the particular attributes on which I have been meditating and the resultant impact on my own life and character. When I focus on his patience, I find patience more evident in my own life. When I meditate on his mercy, my heart is tenderized with mercy. When I gaze into eyes of fire and lean into the eternal passion in his heart, my own heart is ignited. *We become what we behold.*

Too often we try to produce more of the character and nature of God in our lives by controlling our behavior. Certainly we are each fully responsible for our own actions, but becoming more Christ-like isn't something we can attain through human effort. Our very best attempts at "sin management" will always fall short. But as we behold him—the holy One who dwells *within* us—we "*are being transformed into his likeness with ever increasing glory*" (2 Cor.3:18). As Bob Sorge writes in his book, *Secrets of the Secret Place*, "Sin is like cancer. God's presence is radiation on that cancer." The more we meditate on *him*, the more his likeness and character shines through our lives.

Several years ago, I had been offended in some way by an acquaintance. I honestly don't remember the situation itself, but it seemed important at the time. I normally set apart time in the morning to meet with Jesus, but on this particular morning every time I tried to focus on him, instead of meditating on his beauty, I found myself distracted by my hurt feelings.

This went on for a while (for too long) and it was almost time for me to get ready for work. While I still had just a few minutes, I sensed the Lord wooing me back to his presence. I felt pretty sheepish at this point, realizing I had let a little thing snowball into something much bigger and, as a result, my regret was now compounded by the fact that I had missed the opportunity to spend time with Jesus that morning. Still, he persisted in drawing me to himself. As a loving parent might do with a remorseful child ashamed of their behavior, he kept exhorting me to "look at him." Since I had so foolishly wasted my time and emotional energy that morning, it was far easier in that moment to remain downcast and *not* look at him. However, spurred on by his loving patience and grace, I was finally able to look up and gaze directly into those beautiful eyes. When I did, he asked one simple question:

What do you see?

That was all it took. The frost in my heart melted into thankful tears. I knew I was gazing into the eyes of the One who adored me. His gaze held no condemnation — not even the slightest trace of reproof or disappointment — just love and acceptance. Not only was I loved and accepted, he was immensely pleased that I chose to look up rather than remaining trapped in the frustration of my own failure.

Those few short moments of looking to him did two things: First, I was able to immediately release the hurt in my heart and my peace was restored. All the frustration and distraction I felt was instantly evaporated by the love in his eyes. Second, but just as important, almost as soon as I saw the way he was looking at me *I recognized that this is also how he looks upon the person with whom I was so frustrated.* I realized I was angry with someone *he loved.* I knew he desired that I extend grace to my friend as freely as he had extended it to me.

Obviously, every situation isn't quite as easy to overcome and resolve as this example. But even in areas of deep wounding, or areas of besetting sins and strongholds, the single most important thing we can do *is look to him.*

What is *your* need? Are you looking for victory to overcome sin or bondage? Set your gaze upon the victorious Lord of Hosts who wars on your behalf and has never lost a battle. Do you need the grace to forgive? Meditate upon the Redeemer who paid such a great price to forgive you. Do you need resources? Look to Jehovah Jireh, the God who provides.

Healing for a broken heart? Seek the face of the Comforter. The list goes on and on. He is *everything* we need — and more.

Asking in His Name

The more we apprehend the remarkable facets of his character and nature, the more we will begin to grasp how astounding it is that he has chosen to reveal himself to humanity. What is even more unfathomable is that he desires relationship — and even *partnership* — with us. Jesus made an incredible statement in John 14:14, *"You may ask me for anything in my name, and I will do it."* What an amazing invitation! But what does it really mean to ask *in his name*?

In Christian circles we often add "in Jesus' name" to the end of our prayers, but simply adding those words as a tagline does absolutely nothing to guarantee we are truly asking in *his* name. If I showed up at Bill Gates' bank and demanded money in Bill Gates' name, I'm sure I would be shown the door very quickly — if not worse! However, if I was actually *sent* to the bank *by* Bill Gates as his representative, then I would be operating *in his name* and, as a result, I would have his authority. Not to mention a very different experience at the bank!

There have been many, many horrific things done throughout the course of history by people claiming to act in the name of Jesus, but they were *not* acting under his authority. Similarly, there have been many sincere but misguided things prayed by believers throughout the ages "in the name of Jesus" that were *not* prayed in alignment with God's will and purposes. To ask in Jesus' name means to ask as his representative; as his ambassador. When we ask in his name, we ask based on *his* character and *his* desires. We're asking for "his kingdom to come and his will to be done."

Often Christians don't see regular answers to their prayers because we don't pray in alignment with God's heart and purposes. We pray "at" God rather than "with" him. We want to get stuff from God (answers for ourselves and for those we love) instead of primarily desiring to get God himself. It's not that the Lord isn't concerned about our needs and desires—he is and he invites us to come to him with every need—but our own needs and desires shouldn't continually be the *primary* focus of our prayers. When we become captivated by the splendor of Jesus—his character, his nature, his desires—we enter into a higher reality with him. *"If you remain in me and my words remain in you, ask whatever you wish and it will be given to you"* (John 15:7). Jesus longs for us to enter into an abiding place of friendship with him. From that place of intimate friendship, we're invited to not only know what he is doing—but to *join him.*

While our prayer room was open, we had a regular Thursday night prayer meeting with an international focus. One particular Thursday, I was feeling extremely discouraged and was not at all in the mood to be leading a prayer meeting. It was a small group that evening—only our small core group of regulars showed up—and I was glad. We spent way too long chatting (translation: *complaining*) before getting started. Once we finally got going, my prayers sounded whiney and pathetic to my own ears. I was fed up just listening to myself, so I tossed out a challenge to the Lord that went something like this:

"Well Lord, we have a schedule posted that says tonight we are supposed to be praying for the nations. You already know I don't have any desire or ability to do that right now, but this isn't about me, we are here for you. So if there is something *you* want to do tonight and you would like us to join you, we are willing. But you have to help us and show us, otherwise we'll just make it an early night."

As soon as I got the words out of my mouth, the atmosphere in the prayer room shifted. Before we even knew what had happened, the Holy Spirit joined the prayer meeting and we spent well over two hours crying out for the nation of Thailand and for justice for victims of human trafficking. Despite the slow start to the evening and the weakness of our flesh and emotions, we prayed with the confidence and boldness that comes only from asking *in his name.* "Your kingdom come, your will be done, on earth as it is in heaven" wasn't wishful thinking—it was a present tense reality grounded in the certainty we were praying in alignment with the heartbeat of heaven.

Apparently the Lord didn't want me to soon forget the lesson of that evening. Only a week or two later, I received a copy of a news article from Thailand *that provided evidence of a direct answer to a very specific decree we had proclaimed over and over that night.* I already had great confidence that he heard us—proof of the answer was just the icing on the cake. We had prayed as his ambassadors, sent in his name, with his authority—and the things we prayed were accomplished even as the words were spoken.

> *This is the confidence that we have in approaching God: if we ask anything according to his will; he hears us. And if we know he hears us – whatever we ask – we know that we have what we asked of him.* **—1 John 5:14-1**

His name *is* above every other name. Everything in all of creation—including creation itself—is subject to the power of his name. Yet he made himself knowable. He made himself accessible. And he invites *us* to join him in doing the things he is doing.

I started this chapter with the story of the disciples being tossed to and fro in a storm Jesus was sleeping through. The disciples didn't demonstrate much faith that night, but at least they learned something. The next time they were in a boat during a storm, Jesus wasn't in the boat with them but he did come to them—walking on the sea (see Matt. 14:22-33). As Jesus approached them, Peter got out of the boat and joined him on the waves. Sure, we all know Peter took his eyes off Jesus after a moment and started to sink, but don't lose the bigger point—he got out of the boat. *Peter walked on water.* He made sure it was Jesus, then at *his* word, got out of the boat and joined Jesus doing the miraculous. Peter did the impossible in the name of the One who makes all things possible for those who believe.

> *And when they climbed into the boat, the wind died down.*
> *Then those who were in the boat worshiped him, saying,*
> *"Truly you are the Son of God."* –**Matt. 14:32-33**

Quite a different response this time around. Instead of asking "Who is this?" this time, *they knew who it was.* And they worshiped him. Worship is always a good response when we catch a glimpse of who he is.

So who is he? He is the Son of God; the Messiah; the Redeemer; the Desire of Nations; the Lion of the tribe of Judah; the Holy One of Israel; the Ancient of Days; the Alpha and Omega, the First and the Last, the Beginning and End; the Slain Lamb; the Root of David; the Sovereign over all Creation; the Bright and Morning Star; the Worthy One, the Righteous One, the Reigning One; he is Wisdom, he is Peace, he is Truth, and he is Love; he is All in All; he is Faithful and True, the King of kings and the Lord of lords; he spoke the universe into existence and he holds the seven stars in his hand; his hair is white like wool and his eyes blaze like fire; all of creation groans and longs for him; he is the beautiful Bridegroom and he *is* coming again. His name is Jesus—the name above every other name—*this* is my Beloved and *this* is my Friend. What he says we can trust. What he promises he will do.

This is the One who protects us by the power of his name. And when he says we are going to the other side—*in the power of his name*—we can be sure we'll get there!

CHAPTER 7

The Power of Identity

$\mathcal{T}$hey say a picture is worth a thousand words. Many years ago the Lord painted a picture for me that was worth far more than that. In fact, I'd say it was priceless.

I had gone to a Bible study and the leader was talking about the holiness of God. He asked a sort of humorous question: "Has anyone besides me ever felt like pond scum compared to God's holiness?" We all laughed. We laughed partly because it was funny, but even more because we could relate all too well.

A few days later I was driving home from work. Someone cut me off or some other silly thing that I wasn't too happy about and some particularly rotten thought entered my mind. As soon as it did, I sort of chuckled to myself and said, "Yep, pond scum. That would be me." I barely had the words out of my mouth when the Lord opened the eyes of my heart to see an image that is clear to this day.

I saw a beautiful green meadow, complete with a very large pond. All over the surface of the pond was — you guessed it — pond scum. A hand reached down and began to gently scoop away some of the gunk on the water's surface. I knew it was Jesus' hand even before I saw the scars. As he pushed away the pond scum, I could see that the water underneath was beautiful and crystal clear. He leaned over and in that beautiful clear water, I saw his reflection. At that moment, the Lord lovingly spoke to my heart words that I'll never forget:

That's what I see when I look at you — the beauty, the perfection, and the holiness of my Son.

This is the truth of our identity before the throne of Almighty God. We are fully loved and fully accepted, clothed in the righteousness of Christ. We are cherished. As long as we walk on this earth and are living in these bodies of flesh there will often appear to be some "pond scum" on the surface of our lives, but that's not the reality of who we are and it certainly *isn't* what God sees when he looks at us. He sees the beauty of Christ alive in us. Our sin has been paid for and even when we mess up after our salvation, contrary to popular belief, our sin does not necessarily "hurt" or "grieve" God. He hurts *for us* but it doesn't change his opinion of us. He already paid the price for *all* of the "pond scum" in our lives on Calvary. It is finished!

Grasping the revelation that we are clothed in the righteousness of Christ and fully accepted before a holy God is essential to discovering the reality of our identity in Christ, *but it is only the beginning.* We are not only made righteous through the blood of Jesus, we are *co-heirs* with Christ. And even more astounding — we are *his* inheritance. We are the object of his affections and his long-awaited reward. *This* is our identity. But there are forces at work that will do just about anything to keep us from a genuine heart revelation of this truth.

One of the greatest challenges in each of our lives is to simply believe what God says about us. It really is the ultimate in absurdity to disagree with him! Yet it is amazing how often we do. We must make it our goal to learn to walk in the reality of *who we already are.*

Spiritual Identity Theft

The crime of identity theft has been on the rise in the United States for a number of years now. However, it has been occurring in the Church for far longer than that. Satan is a one-trick pony and his only real weapon is the lie. Jesus said the devil is *"a liar and the father of lies"* (John 8:44). Hell's scheme is to get you to believe a lie about God, about yourself, or about others — often all three — with the ultimate goal of discrediting God and stealing the stunning reality of our identity in Christ.

In Hebrew culture, names play a huge role in defining the character and identity of a person. There are many examples throughout Scripture of a person's name being changed after a significant encounter with God that redefined their identity. Abram became Abraham, Jacob became Israel, Saul of Tarsus became the Apostle Paul, just to name a few. One of my favorite name changes is when Jesus changed Simon's name (which means "pebble") to Peter (which means "rock"). Jesus called out who Peter was intended to be long before Peter began to walk in the reality of his true identity.

Name changes from God serve as amazing reminders of who he created us to be, but the "thief" — who wants to steal our God given identity — has been known to attempt a few name changes of his own. When Daniel and his friends were taken into captivity by the Babylonians, (see Daniel 1), they were not only forced to leave their homes and all that was familiar, but they were also given new names by their captors. The name Daniel means "God is my judge," his new name,

Belteshazzar, means "Bel's prince" or "treasured by Bel." Bel was the principle "deity" worshiped by the Babylonians. The name changes for Daniel's three companions— Hananiah was renamed Shadrach, Mishael was renamed Meshach, and Azariah was renamed Abednego—all signified similar shifts from their God given identity to one that suggested allegiance to false gods. But Daniel and his friends weren't buying. They knew *whose* they were and they knew *who* they were, so the labels another kingdom tried to force upon them could not rob them of their true identity. They may have been called something different, but in their hearts *they knew they were who God said they were* and their allegiance was to the true King.

Not much has changed. This world still tries to attach names and labels to us that are contrary to our true identity as beloved sons and daughters of the King. Names like "rejected" "failure" "fearful" "unlovable" are just a few of the false identities this world tries to hang around our necks. But like Daniel, we need to cling to the reality of our true identity because we are "chosen" "victorious" "courageous" and "dearly loved." These words don't describe who we'll become if we work really hard— *they describe who we already are in Christ.*

For many years I lived under the weight of a false identity. Because of several traumatic events in my life as a young person, I began to see myself as a victim. It wasn't the identity I intended to choose for myself, but once its roots were established in my heart and mind, it became familiar and, therefore, difficult to overcome. But as I grew closer to the Lord, I knew I wanted to be whole. More importantly, I began to believe change was possible— *for me.*

Jesus began to heal some of the very deepest areas of my heart, but it wasn't easy. When deep trauma and pain has been buried for a long time, allowing it to be uncovered takes a huge amount of commitment and courage. I was terrified by what I thought I would have to face to be healed, but I determined that no matter what it cost or how long it took, I *would* be whole. I would be who *God* created me to be.

Well, it didn't take years; it took only a moment. In a single encounter with Jesus, he revealed the core lie I had believed about who I was and replaced it with the truth of how *he* saw me. There is a much longer back story that led up to that moment of breakthrough, but the reality is that *in an instant* he delivered me from the false identity "victim" and broke the chains of depression I had struggled with since my teens. I can honestly say I have never thought of myself as a victim again. My stolen identity was recovered and I am victorious in Christ!

Changing Our Minds

My "destination" had been changed when I accepted Jesus as my Savior, but my *destiny* was changed when my identity was restored. My identity was restored *when I agreed with God about who I was* rather than continuing to walk in the false identity created by my experiences and feelings. Once God revealed the truth of my identity from *his* perspective, I needed to break my agreement with the lies I believed and come into agreement with God. Although I had no responsibility for the things done to me, I *was* responsible for my response. Once I knew the truth, I needed to change my mind. Really, I needed to repent. We tend to think of repentance as a change in our behavior or direction, but to truly repent means *to change your mind.*

Although the power of even the most deeply rooted lies can be broken in a moment, learning to walk in the truth of our identity is a lifetime endeavor. None of us has arrived. Only Jesus perfectly demonstrated the reality of walking fully in his identity, but since he did it as a man (see Phil. 2:6-8) he showed us it *is* possible.

Breaking agreement with the lies spoken over and into our lives is the first—and most important—step toward freedom. But even after the lies we believe are exposed and broken we need to continually renew our minds in the truth. There is much taught on Christian disciplines such as prayer, fasting, giving, serving and so on, but one of the most important and often neglected disciplines is that of "taking our thoughts captive to the obedience of Christ" (2 Cor. 10:5 paraphrased). *To walk in truth, our thoughts must be submitted to the truth.*

Not long after I experienced that first, powerful breakthrough in the restoration of my identity, my new reality was tested frequently and fervently. It seemed that circumstances conspired in every way imaginable to convince me it was all my imagination and nothing had really changed. During this time, I read Neil Anderson's book *Victory Over the Darkness: Realizing the Power of Your Identity in Christ.* This book contains a powerful list of statements taken directly from the pages of Scripture that reinforce the reality of our identity. I typed out the Scriptures that were most meaningful to me and read them out loud over myself every single day, sometimes multiple times a day, for months.

After awhile I no longer felt the need to read them daily, but whenever I was feeling particularly weak or vulnerable, I would pull them out and proclaim them again. I didn't really understand the power of what I was doing at the time, but by declaring—*out loud*—who God said I was, I was confronting the lies of the deceiver and renewing my mind in the truth. *"Do not conform any longer to the pattern of this world but be transformed by the renewing of your mind. Then you will be able to test and approve what God's will is—his good, pleasing and perfect will"* (Romans 12:2). God's good, pleasing and perfect will is that we walk in the fullness of what it cost him so dearly to purchase for us.

There is such power in agreement with the truth of God's Word. When we choose to believe our circumstances or feelings above the promises of God, we have put those things in a higher place than him. Who are we to say we know more about who we are than the One who created us? Feelings are just feelings. They are not inherently "bad," but they do sometimes lie.

I once heard it said that feelings are like children—when they're good, enjoy them, but when they misbehave, don't let them rule the house. I thought it was a great analogy but also believed it to be a bit incomplete. The problem with misbehaving feelings is that people often *ignore* them. Well, what happens to misbehaving children when you ignore them? Most of the time they misbehave more! *They want attention*— and so do our misbehaving feelings. When you are sad, it doesn't do a whole lot of good to pretend you are not. You just push the sadness deeper where it will eventually misbehave even more. I have found that a better answer than ignoring our misbehaving feelings is to *discipline* them. We discipline misbehaving feelings by taking them captive to the truth. Acknowledge their presence, but then also acknowledge the greater truth of God's presence and promises even in the midst of less than positive feelings.

We face an ongoing battle for control of our thoughts. The greatest battleground is the one that rages between our ears. What we believe about ourselves defines how we behave. Our greatest weapon in this battle is the truth. Jesus said, *"You will know the truth, and the truth will make you free"* (John 8:32). The importance of *declaring* the truth of who God says we are and what he has promised cannot be over emphasized.

Even after I no longer needed to declare the Scriptures relevant to my identity in Christ daily, I found I did still need to declare promises that were specifically relevant to me and my calling. I started writing out prayers that incorporated Scriptures that were meaningful to me in a particular season and would keep it handy to pull out and pray whenever I felt myself drifting from a place of standing firm in the truth. Here is one example:

Lord,

Thank you for being my light and salvation, whom shall I fear? If you are for me, who can be against me? Thank you, Lord, that greater is he who is in me than he who is in the world. I know that you will never leave me nor forsake me and that you love me with an everlasting love. Nothing can ever separate me from your love! I am my beloved's and he is mine; I am my beloved's and his desire is for me. As a bridegroom rejoices over his bride — my God rejoices over me. You have made known to me the path of life; in your presence is fullness of joy, at your right hand are pleasures forevermore! Surely I have a delightful inheritance. You will perfect that which concerns me and I am confident that he who began this good work in me will carry it out to completion until the day of Christ Jesus. Lord, let your will be done and let your kingdom come in my life! In Jesus' name, Amen

(See Ps. 27:1, Rom. 8:31, 1 John 4:4, Josh.1:5, Jer.31:3, Rom.8:39, Song.6:3 & 7:10, Is.62:5, Ps.16:11, Ps. 16:6, Ps.138:8, Phil. 1:6, Matt.6:10)

God speaks to us as individuals and the Scriptures and promises that are meaningful to *you* may be quite different. The key is to proclaim the truth! Say it, pray it, sing it, write it, and even shout it from the rooftops — we belong to Jesus and he is faithful to his promises and loving toward all he has made!

"I Have Called You Friends"

God's love and intentions toward us will never change, but as we grow in grace our relationship with him does take on different dimensions. Each aspect builds upon the previous stages of relationship and together they combine to form our identity and inheritance in him.

When we're born again, we are spiritual infants. We recognize God the Father as the One who meets our needs. The One who protects us, defends us, and comforts us. While we will *always* be his children—and he will *always* be the One who meets our needs and protects and defends us—after awhile we should begin to mature. A toddler with a bottle is still cute; a twenty-year-old with a bottle is not! Our behavior should begin to grow and change over time. While God will continue to love us even if we never mature, he desires that we grow up *for our own sake.*

As we grow in understanding of the grace we've been given, our perspective begins to shift as we realize everything doesn't revolve around us. Out of deep gratitude, we desire to serve this glorious One who has saved us. For some this realization is almost immediate, for others it may take years. This is when many believers start to find their place in the body. We begin to discover our gifts and abilities and have a desire to use them to further the Kingdom. We become servants to the great Master. As his servants, we never stop being his children, but grateful for all he has done, we gladly pour out our lives to serve him and those he loves. Our hearts become mindful of those *he* desires to reach and we desire to live in obedience to his call.

The journey of many in the Church stops at one of these two stages. Scores have never grown beyond the "child" stage and are still looking to Jesus primarily for what they can get.

They never learn to give away what they've received and, as a result, they stay stuck in the nursery school of faith. Many others *do* learn "it's not about them" and they become faithful servants. In fact, some serve tirelessly their entire lives, but it stops there. All too often, the service itself becomes their identity and they are not able to embrace another level of relationship with Jesus — that of intimate friendship.

When Jesus said to those closest to him, *"I no longer call you servants, because a servant does not know his master's business. Instead I have called you friends for everything I have learned from my Father I made known to you"* (John 15:15), he was revealing a higher level of relationship and identity. In the Old Testament, the Lord revealed the same concept through the prophet Hosea, *"'In that day,' declares the Lord, 'You will call me 'my husband'; you will no longer call me 'master'"* (Hosea 2:16). Jesus invites us into a relationship that moves beyond that of a child or servant and into one of intimacy and partnership. It does not *replace* the other aspects of our relationship with him, it builds upon them.

If becoming a faithful servant was the highest form of relationship with God, he didn't need to create us. He has legions of angels who serve him faithfully. But he wanted more. God desires lovers and confidantes — those who will share his heart.

Jesus isn't returning for children and he isn't returning for servants — he is returning for *a bride* who will rule and reign with him. This remarkable dimension of our identity is a key to walking in the fullness of all he has created us to be. When our identity is secure, so is our destiny.

Since then you have been raised with Christ, set your hearts on things above, where Christ is seated at the right hand of God. Set your minds on things above, not on earthly things. For you died, and your life is now hidden with Christ in God. And when Christ, who is your life, appears, you also will be with him in glory." –**Col. 3:1-4**

We have been raised with Christ. Our lives are hidden with Christ in God. This is *who* we are. This is *where* we are— we are secure in him. We are righteous in him. We are *desired* by him. We are his long awaited reward.

We just need to believe it—*and walk in the reality of who we already are.*

CHAPTER 8

Remembering the Forgotten

*T*his chapter may not be about what you might think it's about. When we think of the forgotten, the last and the least, most often we think of the poor and oppressed; the persecuted and abandoned; the lost and the hopeless. There are many around the globe, even in our own country, who have so little and are suffering in ways that are often unimaginable. Are we, as the Church, doing enough for them? Heavens no! We haven't even begun to scratch the surface in bringing a tangible expression of heaven's love and provision to those in desperate physical and emotional need outside the walls of the local church. And we probably never will—until we deal with our lack *inside* the Church.

When Jesus said, *"None has been lost"* (John 17:12), he was speaking of having protected his own disciples from the evil one. We could use a good dose of that same protectiveness toward the weak, the hurting, the broken, and the lonely in our midst every Sunday morning. While the application of this verse is a bit of a stretch, the principle is still valid. We need to create a culture of compassion, honor, safety—*and family*—

within our own churches before we can expect to shift the culture of entire cities and nations.

A Need is a Need

When I went on my first overseas mission trip to a third world country (Cambodia), I was a little worried about how my heart would fare in coping with some of the circumstances I knew we would face. And sure enough, we did face horrific examples of abject poverty, disease, and even depravity. My heart *did* break and it was extremely difficult. But it was also something else ... *familiar*. In fact, it felt so familiar it was almost a little eerie.

"Have I done this before?"

"Why do I feel like I've been doing this for years?"

"This *is* the first time I've been here, right?"

It may sound silly, but those are the questions I found myself asking the Lord. It wasn't until I returned home that I made the connection. I was praying for the needs of people in my church and as my heart opened before the Spirit of God on their behalf, those same intense feelings of compassion over brokenness and indignation at the injustice of circumstances swept over me. As it did, I understood. In the eyes of the Lord, a need is a need. He doesn't rate broken people on a scale. When you hurt, he hurts. What I experienced in Cambodia was familiar, because having a heart of compassion toward broken, hurting people was familiar.

The needs of those living in poverty and squalor are obvious. The heartache hidden behind the plastic smile of the person sitting in the pew next to you at church is *not* always so obvious. That is not to say that having a broken heart or being spiritually bankrupt is the same issue as not having a roof over your head or food in your belly—obviously it isn't. But if the broken hearts and lives *within* the Church were healed, I would venture to say a lot more would get done for those in need *outside* the Church. The sad irony is that the Church already *has* the keys to unlock answers for every need both inside *and* outside the walls of the church. We have all we need *in* Christ. But a quick glance around reveals an obvious disconnect between how much we have been given and how much we have actually apprehended. We need to get real about this disconnect — in more ways than one.

We need to get real period. I so appreciate people of faith who choose to focus on the positive, but there can be a fine line between faith and denial. Faith is never the denial of reality; it is the presence of a higher and greater reality even in the midst of our humanity, frailty, and brokenness. We will never be able to take the next step in our journey toward wholeness — individually or collectively — if we are deceived into thinking we are already several steps down the road.

I once heard a pastor preach on the many facades we all hide behind. He challenged those listening to ask the Lord to reveal the areas we were trying to be someone or something other than who we authentically were. After listening, I asked Jesus this question: "Is there something I'm trying to be that I'm not?" His reply was gentle, but direct:

Oh, just a little further along than you really are.

Ouch!

What's scary is that I tend to be a bit more real than most! Though I'm usually quite transparent, the Lord has often revealed there are still various filters and pretenses that impact my personal interactions and relationships. It is a huge risk to be *really* real in our overly sanitized "churchianity" culture. Anyone who doesn't think it is has never tried it! We want enough transparency to make us *feel* authentic, but not enough to break through the barriers and lies that keep us from connecting at much deeper levels.

Many of us grew up in environments where stoicism was encouraged and it was never okay to let on that things really weren't all that great. In the Church, this paradigm is greatly intensified by the trappings of religion. The Church is filled with a multitude of people who sincerely believe acknowledging any point of weakness demonstrates a lack of faith. Religion hardwires us with certain mindsets that define spirituality and Christian maturity. If we were to be really honest, most of us believe maturity should look a certain way. But how is that paradigm working out for us?

We're not all wired the same way and we don't all have the same personalities, backgrounds, and experiences. We won't all respond the same way, or in the same timing. Yet we still need to love each other—in word *and* deed. We need to see each other through the Lord's eyes, especially those who seem to have a harder time learning to walk out the reality of their identity in Christ (and even those who *never* walk it out). I'm not talking about embracing an "anything goes" kind of co-dependency that enables or even encourages people to stay broken, but I *am* talking about broadening our perspective beyond our own filters and natural predispositions long enough to realize our personal understanding of any given situation is always limited.

I grew up with different wiring than most of my family. I come from a family of *very* strong-willed people, but I must have missed that gene! I was a right-brained dreamer in a predominantly left-brained household, so I usually saw—*and felt*—things through a different grid. As the "overly-sensitive" one, I wasn't able to shove my feelings down long enough get the "let's pretend everything is great" routine down. It wasn't for lack of trying—I was just made differently. Since I *wasn't* strong (at least not in the same ways), I grew up believing it wasn't okay to be myself.

Not being able to safely express my feelings probably wouldn't have had such a dramatic impact on me if there hadn't been so much heartache early in my life. My father was killed when I was just nine and things started on a downhill spiral from there. My sensitivity is a huge part of who I am, but it also tended to stir things up in my mom that she wasn't well equipped to cope with. I know it was never her intention—she absolutely did the best she could under incredibly difficult circumstances—but since a core part of my personality seemed to frustrate her greatly, I was convinced she didn't think much of me in general. I knew she loved me, but I never thought she *liked* me. On her end, she honestly thought I was being rebellious and trying to make things difficult for her. If I had been in her shoes, I may have drawn the same conclusion, but nothing could have been further from the truth. I wasn't trying to upset the applecart; I simply wasn't *able* to respond the way she wanted me to.

Really, most of the behavior my mom interpreted as rebellious was aimed at one thing: I wanted to be heard and understood. We *all* have that need. It is not wrong to have needs. We are relational beings created for healthy, vibrant relationship with God and each other. But sometimes—because we are not able to recognize or admit many of our needs, or often simply because we are broken people trying to love other broken people—those very real needs remain unmet in our lives.

Long before I ever felt like anyone else heard me—Jesus did. To this day, I am amazed by how compassionate and patient he is with me. He always knows what I need even when I don't know myself. Although I had to learn (as discussed in the previous chapter) to take my "misbehaving" feelings captive to the truth, the Lord has *never* denied me the right to feel. Even when I've expected him to tell me to "pull myself up by my bootstraps and get it together" he never has. Since rebellion isn't typically at the root of my actions, addressing me in a strong, corrective manner is rarely helpful. However, while I don't tend toward willful rebellion, I *do* have significant weaknesses in a number of areas. Many times, I have been *unable* to respond differently to circumstances—not *unwilling*. And from God's perspective, that is a dynamically different issue.

The Lord underscored his compassion and understanding of my emotions in a surprising way many years ago. I had just begun serving in a ministry for single moms. I was helping with a special event and the entire week of the event I felt like I was getting beat up one wall and down the next. I was not feeling particularly loved or affirmed from *any* direction. As worship began the night of our meeting, I was broken and spent. The worship leader began singing and in the safety of God's presence, the dam in my heart burst. I poured my heart out to Jesus and found myself complaining to him that I did not feel loved. As soon as that plaintive cry escaped my lips, I saw a picture of Jesus on the cross and instantly felt incredibly ashamed of my whimpering. After all he did for me for the sake of love—who was I to not *feel* loved? As I contemplated the demonstration of his great love, I was expecting to hear a gentle rebuke for my unbelief and lack of perspective, but instead he said something that absolutely shocked me:

I know just how you feel, beloved. I didn't feel loved either.

No exhortation to quit whining and get it together. No backlash for my lack of gratitude. No conviction, and certainly no condemnation. Just compassion and comfort. *He knew how I felt.* He *cared* how I felt. Despite his great suffering and sacrifice, he thought *my* suffering—though so ridiculously small in comparison—was important and he wanted me to know it.

I've never forgotten that and never will. That sweet moment of validation and understanding spoke volumes to my hurting heart and had far more impact than even the very gentlest rebuke could ever have had. He knew my need wasn't to be corrected—my feelings had been corrected my entire life—my need was to be heard and understood. To him, my needs weren't small and unimportant; they were valid and very, very important to him.

In his eyes, a need is a need. When we hurt, so does he. *"Praise be to the God and Father of our Lord Jesus Christ, the Father of compassion and God of all comfort, who comforts us in all our trouble so we can comfort those who are in any trouble with the comfort we ourselves have received from Chris"* (2 Cor.1:3-4). When we acknowledge our own needs and receive of his great comfort, we become equipped to comfort others. But if we never acknowledge we have needs, we never receive comfort and don't have much of anything to give. No need is unimportant in his eyes—not our own; not those of our brothers and sisters. Oh, how we need to learn to see each other with *his* eyes of compassion! What an incredible difference it would make.

The Loneliness Epidemic

There is one need in particular that has grown like a cancer in our midst. It is no respecter of persons. It affects young and old, male and female, mature and immature—it seems no one is immune. It has reached epidemic proportions in our society. Its name? Loneliness.

Western culture honors independence. Unlike many other cultures, we are not dependent upon each other to survive. Instead, we celebrate the survival of the fittest. We often unconsciously view relationships in terms of their usefulness, rather than in terms of commitment and love. With the advent of technologies such as texting, Skype, Twitter, and other types of social media, the breadth of our relationships and sphere of influence has increased dramatically in recent years, but the *depth* of our relationships is sorely lacking. How deeply can you *really* connect to 500 friends on Facebook? We are busier than ever, but connecting in deep and meaningful ways less and less often.

Just as we have experienced a breakdown of family in our society, we have also experienced a breakdown of family in the Church. The Church was never intended to be an institution. It was intended to be a living, breathing organism that provides the foundation for authentic spiritual community and family. But in our emphasis on gathering around doctrinal ideas and programs, *we've lost the emphasis on family*.

Most churches are aware of the problem on some level and there has been a lot of talk in recent years on how to build genuine community. In fact, that actually has become part of the problem—there is a lot of *talk*. Most of our attempts to increase social interaction and to include people are well intended, but woefully lacking understanding into the true heart of the issue.

For the most part, our "solutions" put the burden squarely on the backs of the people who can bear it the least—the ones who are truly lonely. An orphaned child doesn't become part of a family after they try real hard to connect and reach out—they become part of a family when *they are adopted*. A huge part of that comes, of course, from understanding our adoption into God's family. But the Church is supposed to be a practical, flesh and blood expression of God's family. And in that we have failed—miserably.

You don't create a sense of family for those who are alone simply by meeting in a small group once week or occasionally sharing a meal together. Those things are a beginning, a place of opportunity, but they bring us to the "outer court" of relationship, not into an "inner circle." It's not a matter of simply sharing a meal together—it is a matter of sharing our *lives* with one another. Sharing life doesn't happen when several people get together in a room for an hour or two each week and then run off in a zillion different directions and go their separate ways for the rest of the week.

It's also not a matter of simply healing the individual. Bringing greater healing and freedom to individuals is an essential part of the picture, but it is still only a piece of the whole. If you put a healthy finger onto a hand with gangrene it won't be long before the finger starts exhibiting symptoms of the same disease. When you put a healed person back into a broken system, they will never fully flourish.

I'm convinced that part of our failure lies in our perception of the problem. People often assume that a need in this area is the result of choices or the result of some ultimate lack of faith or trust in God. Is it sometimes? Sure. But even then it is still only a small part of the whole. Don't assume a person without ties to a strong community is perpetuating the problem and that the situation is solely the result of their own choices. Sometimes loneliness is simply a circumstance—not a character flaw or sin. Acknowledging it does not make a person excessively needy; it makes them human. In the Garden of Eden, Adam was walking in perfect unbroken fellowship with God, yet in the midst that perfect setting, God said it wasn't good for Adam to be alone. It still isn't good for people to be alone.

I have been single for many years and, since my children are grown, I live alone. Even though I am blessed with some of the most amazing friends on the planet, including a few cherished long-term relationships, we are all busy with many things. As a result, I have been extremely lonely during certain seasons of life. Even when you know lots of great people, if your schedules and commitments aren't in sync, you don't have anyone to "do life" with. Despite frequent efforts to reach out and connect with new people, it has, at times, been quite wearying and discouraging.

During these seasons, one of the hardest things to bear has been the added burden of a culture that reinforces the idea that somehow I have created my circumstances and that I alone have the responsibility for making the situation better. I am responsible for my *response* to circumstances (and for keeping my own heart alive and open to love), but I can't "fix" a problem that extends far beyond the impact to my own life.

Like me, many of those I know in similar situations aren't looking for anyone to swoop in with a magic bullet to fix things. For the most part, we are simply looking for understanding and *acknowledgement that a genuine problem exists* (in our culture *and* in our churches)—a problem that can't be solved by simply joining one more group or reaching out to one more person.

The body as a whole is far more broken than the individual pieces, but we tend to view the problem as if it were the other way around. That actually *is* at the heart of the problem—we are individual pieces and we don't know how to come together to make the whole. This isn't just an individual issue—*it's our issue*—and we will never resolve it without coming to terms with our deep areas of corporate lack.

Again, I don't know how to fix that. In fact, I *can't* fix it. We can only fix it *together* under the specific leadership of the Holy Spirit. *"God sets the lonely in families"* (Ps.68:6). Ultimately it's his work and not something we can force. But we can be honest. We can be sensitive. We can be aware. We can be *real* — which means admitting our collective lack and our failure. The first step is to quit denying there *is* a problem and to stop blaming the individual pieces. It's not my problem. It's not your problem. *It's our problem.* And it is woven deeply into the very fabric of our culture.

Heaven has solutions, but we need to start asking the right questions. Though it is a bigger and more complex problem than most of us would like to acknowledge, I believe the Lord is highlighting this issues to many people in this season for one reason — he wants to do something.

> *God has arranged the parts in the body, every one of them, just as he wanted them to be. If they were all one part, where would the body be? As it is, there are many parts, but one body. The eye cannot say to the hand, "I don't need you!" And the head cannot say to the feet, "I don't need you!" On the contrary, those parts of the body that seem to be weaker are indispensable, and the parts that we think are less honorable we treat with special honor. And the parts that are unpresentable are treated with special modesty, while our presentable parts need no special treatment. But God has combined the members of the body and has given greater honor to the parts that lacked it, so that there should be no division in the body, but that its parts should have equal concern for each other. If one part suffers, every part suffers with it; if one part is honored, every part rejoices with it.* –1 **Corinthians 12:18-26**

If one part of the body suffers, we all suffer. As long as there are pieces that are hurting and broken, or pieces that are lonely and out of place, we are incomplete. He has created each of us uniquely and each of us is designed to fulfill a critical role in the overall function of the body. When even one member is out of place, we are less than we were designed to be. *We need each other.* When we finally deal with the lack inside the Church, we'll be much better equipped to deal with the lack outside the Church.

For our sake — for their sake — for *his* sake — I pray that not one will be lost or forgotten.

CHAPTER 9

Fullness of Joy

It had been a long week. Every Friday evening a group of us gathered in my living room to seek the Lord through worship, prayer, Bible study, and fellowship. This particular week there was a profound sense of heaviness in the air and our prayers didn't seem to be going any higher than the ceiling. One woman in the group needed to drive out to Hesperia (a town a good distance away) that night to visit a family member. It was a long drive, so she got ready to leave a bit early. She was probably glad to have an early escape!

Like the rest of us, Juanita was already *very* tired so I wanted to pray for her before she got on the road. I put my hand on her shoulder and started praying with the utmost sincerity and seriousness.

I never got past the first sentence.

"Oh Lord, please watch over Juanita and give her traveling mercies as she drives out to *Hysteria* ...."

The word hung in the air for a split second. Of course I meant to say *Hesperia,* but it didn't come out that way. After a second, as if on cue, we all simultaneously burst into fits of uncontrollable laughter. We laughed and laughed and laughed for what seemed like hours. I'm not sure I had ever laughed so hard in my life. My daughter, who was a teenager at the time, wasn't in on the joke and was *not* amused. From time to time she would come out of her room, look down the stairs with an annoyed look on her face as if to say "Still?" then roll her eyes as she stomped back into her room and slammed the door. Each time she did — it set us off again.

It took a long time for Juanita to get on the road to Hesperia that night, but it only took a few seconds for all of us to make the trip to *Hysteria.* And what a trip it was! Although the week had been filled with obstacles and challenges, a single outbreak of spontaneous joy broke the heaviness that had hung over us all night and completely shifted the atmosphere in the room and in our hearts. Laughter *is* good medicine!

The Healing Power of Joy

"A cheerful heart is good medicine, but a crushed spirit dries up the bones" (Proverbs 17:22). The medical community has long understood the healing power of laughter. Laughter not only reduces stress, but actually increases brain chemistry, improves circulation, and in general increases oxygenation in the body which has a whole host of positive physical benefits. Mike Adams, author of *The Five Habits of Health Transformation* estimates that a minute of laughter is worth $10,000 in bio-chemicals:

> *"Your body manufactures chemicals based on certain needs and then distributes them throughout your body. When you laugh, you generate a wealth of healing bio-*

chemicals. I've often stated that for every minute of laughter, you produce somewhere around $10,000 worth of healthy body chemistry, and what I mean is that if you had to go out and actually purchase these refined chemical compounds from labs or pharmaceutical companies, you would have to pay at least $10,000 for the very same chemistry that your brain is producing free of charge when you engage in laughter.

Some of these are brain-altering chemicals such as serotonin; others are immune-boosting chemicals such as interleukins. If you were to make a long list of all the chemicals created by engaging in healthy laughter, you would have quite a list of healthy body chemicals that would carry a hefty price tag if you purchased them retail. And yet, once again, you can create these chemicals for yourself at no cost by simply engaging in laughter.

Laughter benefits our emotional well-being as powerfully as it does our bodies. The night we laughed our way to "Hysteria," our outlook was changed in an instant. Our emotional well-being was restored as heaviness was replaced by joy and hope, literally in a moment. Our moods were altered faster and more completely than any amount of discussion, commiseration, or even prayer could have achieved. The more we laughed, the deeper our hearts and spirits were impacted and renewed.

If something is so obviously good for us, why is laughter so controversial in the Church? The Church should be filled with the happiest, most joy-filled, and hopeful people on earth. We have been given the gift of life — *abundant life* — here and now *and* for all of eternity. Yet joy — true, abiding joy — is one of the most lacking characteristics of the Church. In most churches in North America, anything more than a few seconds of polite laughter at the pastor's bad jokes is considered out of order and bad form. Judging from their countenances, many folks within the walls of some of our local churches seem to think it is more spiritual to look like they've been sucking on lemons than it is to outwardly manifest any evidence of joy!

A few years after my little trip to "Hysteria," I was at an evening service at a local church. The night had been set aside as a time of extended worship and as an opportunity for those who wanted to grow in the understanding and application of the gifts of the Spirit. On this particular night they called people forward for prayer. I was standing next to a friend — "Carrie" — and someone prayed for a release of joy. The next thing I knew, the two of us were on the floor convulsed in fits of laughter. We were laughing so hard we were crying. Each time we thought we had composed ourselves something would set us off again. I should mention that this was *not* typical behavior in this particular church. While many other people seemed to catch the joy, others didn't quite know what to make of the situation.

Every now and then I would catch the eye of one of the staff members — I'll call her Donna — who was watching us with curiosity. I didn't know Donna terribly well, but I *did* know she came from a fairly conservative church background. I could tell we were stretching the boundaries of her comfort zone, but she didn't make any effort to leave or move to a quieter area, she just stayed and watched. In one of those "God moments" you couldn't plan if you tried, Carrie and I stopped laughing at the exact same moment and reached toward Donna to pray. We laid our hands on her and began to prophesy and pray over her. Immediately, it was clear that the Lord was ministering to some very deep areas of her heart. The three of us laughed — and cried — together as God brought strength to her spirit and a deeper revelation of his love to her heart.

We never did talk with Donna about our little "giggle-fest," but I heard through the church grapevine that the evening may have been a bit of a turning point for Donna in allowing the Holy Spirit to move in her life in new ways. Carrie is the wife of one of the pastors on staff and I had been involved in quite a lot of ministry at this particular church, so she knew us well enough to know she couldn't dismiss us as slightly off-balance eccentrics who didn't know how to control themselves. Since the Holy Spirit was so obviously present when we prayed for her, our time of ministry further confirmed we were not "crackpots," but rather sincere followers of Jesus who were experiencing an authentic revelation of God's joy she had not tasted ... *yet*.

God himself is filled with joy and gladness. Zephaniah 3:17 declares not only that he "takes great delight" in us, but also that he "rejoices over (us) with singing." Jesus was "full of joy through the Holy Spirit" (Luke 10:21), and in John 17:13 Jesus prayed that the full measure of *his* joy would be in *us*. In Galatians 5:22-23 of the nine characteristics that demonstrate the fruit of the Spirit, joy is second, right behind love. Joy is an important attribute of the character and nature of God. It should be an important part of our character and nature too.

Joy as a Weapon

Joy *is* a characteristic that all Christians should manifest, but it is also so much more. A friend recently shared a dream he had. He was in a room full of incredibly sick and broken people — those with crippling arthritis and other devastating diseases. As they came to him for prayer, instead of praying — he laughed. As he did, they were all healed.

Joy isn't just good medicine and good for our hearts and souls — it is also one of our most powerful weapons of warfare. God himself demonstrate this principle in the second Psalm:

Why do the nations conspire and the peoples plot in vain? The kings of the earth take their stand and the rulers gather together against the LORD and against his Anointed One. "Let us break their chains," they say, "and throw off their fetters." The One enthroned in heaven laughs. The LORD scoffs at them. –**Psalm 2:4**

It appears that the first reaction of heaven to the threats of the enemy is to simply laugh them off! It really *is* quite absurd to think that anyone or anything could stand against our God or thwart his purposes. When challenges and obstacles are looked at from heaven's perspective, the schemes of hell really are quite laughable.

We have all faced circumstances that are not the least bit funny and I am certainly not implying that we should laugh *at* people in pain or difficult circumstances. But it *is* quite a powerful thing to learn to rejoice *in spite* of the difficulties we face. Joyful people are resilient people. Joy and laughter may not take away the pain of the very real disappointments and heartbreaks of life, but they certainly do make them more bearable! And sometimes joy does even more.

Sometimes it is the very act of rejoicing itself that breaks the chains that bind us to fear and hopelessness. When Paul and Silas were imprisoned in Philippi (see Acts 16:22-34), they had been severely beaten and flogged. As if that weren't enough, their feet were bound in stocks and they were kept in the darkest inner part of the prison. Yet "around midnight," at the darkest hour of the night, in the midst of their deepest suffering, Paul and Silas decided to have a praise party. As they rejoiced, the prison was shaken and their chains were broken. Even more amazing, the prison doors opened, creating a path to freedom for *all* the captives.

Joy still brings freedom to captives. I don't imagine anything frustrates our adversary quite like a saint's joyful trust in God in the midst of sorrow and suffering. If the Lord in heaven laughs when the nations rage against him, maybe we should learn from that. Maybe sometimes we just need to look straight at the obstacles in our lives and say, "Ha, ha! As if you can stop the plans of my God!" — and then have a good laugh. It's not always easy, but it *is* powerful. Even more importantly, learning to laugh at the absurdity of hell's schemes in our lives is often the first step toward learning to authentically rejoice *in the midst* of them.

Finally, Rejoice

Of course joy isn't just about laughing. Laughter is simply one expression of joy. True joy is an attitude of the heart. Even when we don't feel happy or joyful, we *can* maintain the heart position of a joy-filled life.

"We tend to forget that happiness doesn't come as a result of getting something we don't have, but rather of recognizing and appreciating what we do have." I'm not sure where this quote came from, but it is so true. I mentioned in Chapter 4, the link between gratitude and perspective. A line from an old Twila Paris song has often run through my mind and heart: *"Could the joy of life be found in simple gratitude; and is gratitude as simple as perspective?"* The longer I live, the more I am sure the answer to that question is a simple and profound yes!

Since *no one* ever feels happy 24/7, 365 days a year, happy people don't make that their goal. Happiness does not mean living in denial of the trials of life, instead it means learning to live *above* them. The happiest people I know *aren't* the ones who live the most trouble free lives; that certainly wasn't the case for Paul and Silas! Happy people aren't necessarily the ones with the most money or the best jobs. They're not the ones with perfect families, perfect relationships, or perfect health. In fact, if you look beyond the surface of any of their lives, you will find every bit as much heartache — sometimes even more — than the average person. But what they do have is gratitude — *and* perspective.

The Bible actually has quite a lot to say about joy. I particularly love the book of Philippians because it is a real world kind of book. It's not lofty theology; it's practical application for an attitude of gratitude. It's the demonstration of overcoming joy in the midst of the trials of life. Lately my eyes have been drawn to a few short words in the very first verse of the third chapter: *"Finally, my brothers, rejoice in the Lord."* Really, for me it has boiled down to just two of those words: Finally ... rejoice.

And that's what I'm learning to do — finally, rejoice. It hasn't come easily or naturally to me. It does to some people. There are those who are naturally wired with sunny optimistic dispositions. I'm not one of them. I've always been a deep thinker and feeler; that "melancholy" bent is just a natural part of who I am. I've never been good at denial and I can't fake happy. But while I can't fake it — *I've learned I can choose it.* I can purpose to focus on what's good. I can focus on what I have, rather than on what I don't have. I can laugh whenever I'm able to laugh and enjoy every single moment I'm able to enjoy. As I've learned to do these things, a funny thing has happened — genuine joy has become a much more consistent and real characteristic of my life. Not constant, but real and frequent.

After I began writing this particular chapter, many circumstances transpired that have caused me to be anything but joyful. In fact, the past few weeks have been amongst the most sobering I have faced in some time. Joy has not been a *natural* response or emotion during this time. Things have been difficult not only for me, but even more, for those I love dearly. There is a lot going on that is heartbreaking — things I just don't get — and it has been an ongoing battle not to give in to discouragement. I've been telling the Lord I could use just a little bit of encouragement or some good news here and there, but at the moment I am writing these words, nothing much has changed. But in re-reading what I had previously written, I realized that something significant has changed — *me*.

What I mean is this: I *believe* what I wrote. It's real — and not just on good days. My emotions lately have been just that, my emotions. But my heart *is* still happy and content in him. As hard as the past few weeks have been, I *haven't* lost my joy. It hasn't always been hanging out on the surface of my emotions, to be sure, but that is because it has been one of those seasons where I recognize I can't feel happy all the time. What I *have* been able to do, though, is lay hold of every moment that has been good and ride it for all it's worth! I've needed each and every light moment and every single second of laughter I've been able to grab onto. Of course I wish there were more of those moments lately, but there will be again. I'm sure of it. I've changed, *but God hasn't*. He is still reigning in absolute sovereign control over the Universe. He isn't stressed. He isn't worried. He isn't surprised and he hasn't been caught off guard. He knows the end of the story. And he is still filled with joy and gladness. As Bill Johnson is famous for saying, "I've got good news. God's in a good mood!"

Do you believe it? I do. I believe it more than ever. That most certainly does not mean that everything in this world is good. And it absolutely doesn't mean God "approves" of evil or of the bad things that hurt us and cause heartache on this fallen planet. He felt (and feels) our pain so keenly that he made provision for those things through his own blood. But it *is* finished! That's *great* news no matter what else is going on in the world. *"I consider that our present suffering is not worth comparing with the glory that will be revealed in us"* (Romans 8:18). This is *not* the end of the story. But we do know how it *will* end and that fact alone is worth rejoicing over now and for all of eternity.

James said to *"consider it pure joy"* when we face trials because trials test our faith and produce perseverance (see James 1:2-3). As we've already discussed, we *need* perseverance to finish the race. Trials don't rob our joy; unbelief robs our joy. The trials of life actually give us the opportunity to refine and demonstrate our faith. It's all a matter of perspective—and I want heaven's perspective.

Joy is the fruit of the Spirit and joy is the will of God for our lives. Joyful people make God's heart happy. They tend to get along better and make each other happy too—they want to see the best in each other. Joy is an incredibly contagious emotion. I guess that's why people who spend time hanging out with Jesus ultimately end up with a lot of joy in their hearts. When Jesus prayed for the full measure of his joy to be within us (John 17:13), he was inviting us to share the contagious joy of heaven. In case you haven't realized it yet, heaven is a mighty joyful place. God isn't offering a trickle here and there, but abounding joy that springs up from deep wells within us. Abounding joy that flows out to one another. Abounding joy that gives a sorrowful and anxious world a desperately needed glimpse of a good and glad God.

Abounding joy that enables the broken to see the One who gives us *"A crown of beauty instead of ashes, the oil of gladness instead of mourning, and the garment of praise, instead of a spirit of despair"* (Isaiah 61:3). Abounding joy that *"wipes every tear from our eyes"* (see Rev. 21:4). And abounding joy that *"turns our mourning into dancing and takes off our sackcloth and clothes us with gladness"* (Ps 30:11). Jesus has deposited his own joy in us, that our joy may be complete (see John 15:11).

You don't need to go to "Hysteria" to taste the joy and goodness of God, but a trip there now and then doesn't hurt! Laughter *is* good medicine. If God laughs at the threats of the evil one—so can we. *"If God is for me, who can be against me?"* (Romans 8:31). And if the joy of life is found in simple gratitude, and gratitude is as simple as perspective—then we can purpose to focus on what's good. *"Whatever is true, whatever is noble, whatever is right, whatever is pure, whatever is lovely, whatever is admirable–if anything is excellent or praiseworthy, think about such things* (Phil. 4:8).

And *finally*—rejoice.

CHAPTER 10

Sent Into the World

*A*rt was half asleep, curled up in the corner of the rail car when we got on. He opened his eyes and gave a slight nod to my friend in a half-hearted greeting when we sat down near him. Since we were sharing a very small space, we engaged in some friendly small talk. He was clearly tired—we learned he had been working a night shift nearby and was now heading home—but he was still pleasant. At least he was at first.

"Where are you ladies headed?" he asked.

We were on our way to a large, all-day prayer event at a local stadium and told him as much. Apparently that was the wrong answer! In a split second his demeanor changed from one of mildly polite interest to one of barely contained rage. He certainly wasn't sleepy anymore.

"Oh! You're with those right-winged weirdoes!"

I tried to laugh it off. "Well, we're not all *that* weird ..."

He cut me off. "Yes you are! Yes you are! You're one of *those* weirdoes!"

And with that, he launched into a full-scale verbal tirade predominantly centered on what he viewed as the Church's misguided efforts to legislate morality. The diatribe continued until we reached our destination. I don't think he ever took a breath. Since I was the one who responded to his initial assessment of our political and religious leanings, his fury was mostly directed at me. I just listened since it was clear he wouldn't be able to hear anything I had to say anyway.

When we reached our stop and got up to leave, he stopped as suddenly as he began. As I was exiting, I turned around and held out my hand. I wasn't sure what he would do, but to my surprise he accepted the gesture and we parted with a handshake. I knew I didn't have time to say much, but I wanted to somehow acknowledge I had really heard him, so I leaned over and quietly made one simple comment:

"Art, you would be very surprised to know just how much I agree with you."

With that, we left him with his mouth hanging open as we got off the train and headed over to our "right-wing weirdo" event.

In the World But Not of It? What On Earth Does it Mean?

Of course, I didn't agree with *everything* Art said, but I really did agree with most of it. At the heart of his rant was his hatred of hypocrisy. Basically he felt we (the Church) had no right telling other people how to live since he didn't see most Christians living the life they preached. He made it quite clear he personally had seen very little of the love of Jesus demonstrated by those who claimed to follow him and that if we wanted "converts" we might want to try loving people rather than trying to force people to accept our ideals. He was absolutely right.

When Jesus prayed for his disciples he said:

"I have given them your word and the world has hated them, for they are not of the world anymore than I am of the world. My prayer is not that you take them out of the world but that you protect them from the evil one. They are not of the world, even as I am not of it." **–John 17: 14-16**

His desire was that we would remain *in* the world as his ambassadors, but at the same time he made it clear that we were no longer *of* the world. Although we must remain in the world *to spread the influence of the true King and his kingdom,* our citizenship is in heaven. As citizens of heaven, we should reflect heaven's values and not be influenced by the values of the world. Sadly, in many ways it appears we have gotten this exactly backwards — and the "Arts" of the world have noticed.

It's one thing to be hated for living a righteous life, it's quite another to be hated for the hypocrisy of preaching one lifestyle and living another. According to the Barna Group the divorce rate within the Church is virtually indistinguishable from overall national averages. From all appearances, we don't fare much better in areas of depression, alcoholism, infidelity, addiction to pornography, etc. Who is influencing who?

At the same time, instead of invading the world with the love of God, we attempt to draw "outsiders" to our sheltered little corner (the local church) by trying to make it more user-friendly and appealing. We want to entice them to join the club! Sometimes our services are so seeker-sensitive that we completely forget to be *Spirit*-sensitive. What are we thinking? We want to be careful not to offend a non-believer when they step into *God's house*, yet we appear to have absolutely no problem offending God. We change our behavior for the benefit of seekers on *our* turf (the Church), but then we want to tell them how to live on *theirs* (the world)? How did we get this so backwards?

The Church should be spreading a message of hope and life throughout all segments of society by providing the world with an accurate representation of Jesus. By and large, we have failed in achieving this mandate. I once heard it said, "The Church has become an island of irrelevance in a sea of hopelessness." Many parts of the church have become little more than "holy clubs" — concerned more with preserving the gospel of the American dream and making converts to a system of belief, than in being an incarnational presence of Jesus to the world around us. As a result, rather than being seen as having the answers, we've simply become irrelevant. And with good reason! For the most part we don't seem to be faring much better than the world. We actually look worse in some ways, since many of the differences people do see are not necessarily perceived as good. Sadly, many see the Church in North America just as Art does — a bunch of finger-pointing, hypocritical, and incredibly fearful, "right-winged" weirdoes.

Our assignment in this world is to be joy-filled ambassadors proclaiming the love, hope, and *power* of another kingdom. We were never supposed to *go* to church and win converts to the institution; we are supposed to *be* the Church and make disciples of *nations*. Jesus loves his Church immensely, but he also loves the world. As Ralph Winter says, "Until the Church cares more about the future of the world than it cares about the future of the Church, the Church has no future." We are stressed, depressed, and fearful of anything that might rock the boat, because all too often our focus is on preserving a safe and comfortable "kingdom" of our own making. What happened to seeking first *his* kingdom? If we were to be brutally honest, even many of our outreach efforts are focused more on advancing our political and social agenda than they are on advancing the kingdom of God.

All of this points to a Church that is far too often *of* the world, but not *in* it. We reflect the same problems and are influenced by the same temptations and issues of the culture around us, but for the most part we have *not* influenced the world with the ways of the kingdom. If we ever want to see "his kingdom come and his will be done, on earth as it is in heaven" this *must* change.

Jesus was the ultimate example of being in the world but not of it. He absolutely defied the systems of the world (especially the religious systems), but he always consistently and accurately reflected heaven's values. He related to and engaged people in all walks of life, often to the chagrin of the religious establishment, but he never compromised his message or lifestyle. He was a thermostat—he set the climate—rather than a thermometer that simply reflected the current temperature.

People were drawn to Jesus because he welcomed and accepted them. He valued them—the outcasts, the rejects, the sinners, the poor, the oppressed—and he gave them hope. He met people where they were, on their own turf, and he loved them into a revelation of who he was and what he was like. He didn't tell them to go clean up their act before they could hang out with him. Although he stood firmly for what was right, his focus wasn't on advancing a social or political agenda—he simply invited people into his presence. When challenged about paying taxes, which the Jews considered unlawful, Jesus made a clear distinction between the world's systems and God's kingdom when he said to "give to Caesar what is Caesar's and to God, what is God's" (Mark 12:27). He never confused the two worlds. He was in the world, but definitely not of it.

Loving Sinners—Not Sin

Most of us have heard the expression "love the sinner and hate the sin," but we don't appear to be very successful at actually putting this concept into practice. For far too long, the Church's "hatred of sin" has trickled over onto the people who are bound by those sins—*especially certain sins*. People engaged in lifestyles many Christians find offensive don't even bother seeking God in the local church anymore because they fear our judgment and wrath.

In response to this, something of a counter-culture has arisen in recent years that attempts to value love above all. The intention is great, but in many cases it has become a very deficient and sometimes even dangerous kind of "love" due to the complete absence of truth. Out of a very sincere zeal to love and embrace those rejected by the Church for so long, some in the Church have attempted to redefine morality. Instead of drawing attention to the *many* legitimate areas of gray, they have eliminated *all* black and white. The end result is justifying and condoning sin itself.

Most often, it seems we hate the sin and also reject and condemn the sinner (which, by the way, includes all of us since "all have sinned and fall short of the glory of God")—or we love the sinner and also accept and justify the sin. Both miss the mark and fail to reflect the example of grace *and* truth that Jesus set.

When the Pharisees brought the woman caught in adultery to Jesus in an attempt to trap him, he beat them at their own game (John 8:1-11). Jesus did *not* break the law—*he revealed the hypocrisy of how the law was being applied.* On the other hand, though Jesus refused to condemn the woman (whose sin was no greater than the sin of those who set her up) he also wasn't "okay" with her lifestyle. His parting exhortation to her was to go and *leave* her life of sin.

The Woman at the Well (see John 4) was an outcast even amongst her own marginalized culture, but Jesus rejected local prejudices when he went out of his way to meet her *where he knew she would be*. Yet his desire to be with her didn't keep him from pointing out some very difficult truths about her lifestyle.

Jesus enjoyed supper at the home of the tax-collector, Zacchaeus (Luke 19:1-10) without requiring him to make a single change in his lifestyle or behavior, but it was only after Zacchaeus offered to make restitution for his past unethical choices that Jesus made the exclamation, *"Today salvation has come to this house, because this man, too, is a son of Abraham. For the Son of Man came to seek and save the lost."*

Jesus *does* love and accept *all* people, regardless of whether they make any effort to change their lifestyle or behavior. We ought to do the same. *But he still hates sin.* God doesn't hate sin because he is a cosmic kill-joy or the ultimate "Rule-Meister" — he hates sin because it destroys us and it keeps us from his best and highest purposes for our lives.

Ultimately, only God's judgments are righteous. He is the only one able to make an accurate assessment of any individual life. We never have the full story and would be wise to remember that when tempted to judge another person's lifestyle or choices. Obviously it's not difficult to recognize that certain behaviors are inconsistent with a holy life, but we still have no right to judge *the person*. We have no way of knowing how *we* might have responded if we had been faced with the exact same life situations as many of those we so easily condemn. Given the exact same circumstances, it is entirely possible we may have slipped just as far — if not farther — into the same sins. As mentioned in Chapter 8, weakness is *not* the same thing as open, willful rebellion. Yes, there *are* consequences for certain actions. Forgiveness and grace does *not* mean there are no consequences for our behavior and choices. But in the final analysis, only God and the person involved know fully when and where they had the tools and opportunity to choose differently and when and where they did not. We draw conclusions based on what we see on the surface of things; God always sees the heart.

> *"He will not judge by what he sees with his eyes, or decide by what he hears with his ears; but with righteousness he will judge the needy, with justice he will give decisions for the poor of the earth."* – **Isaiah 11:4**

That knowledge should be both reassuring *and* sobering for all of us.

The Church of the Older Brother?

Many sins we associate with worldliness are obvious — things like sexual immorality, theft, drunkenness, etc. — but what about some of the less obvious sins hidden *within* the Church? What about sins like bitterness, envy, gossip, complaining, self-righteousness, or having a critical, judgmental heart? The outward consequences of these sins may be different, but if they continue unchecked and become a lifestyle, their effect on our relationship with the Lord can be every bit as devastating. That's why God hates all sin — not just the ones *we* hate.

Almost everyone is familiar with the well known parable of the prodigal son (Luke 15:11-32). What many fail to grasp is that the story is about *two* lost sons — *not just one*. The younger son's "lost-ness" is painfully obvious, he was lost in the ways of world. But the older brother was every bit as lost. The older brother was lost in self-righteousness *within* the walls of his father's house … also known as the Church.

Ironically, the depth of the older brother's distance from his father's heart wasn't revealed until the younger son came home. When the father rejoiced in welcoming this lost one home without any conditions, the older brother was furious. What?! You mean this sluggard who squandered his inheritance was able to waltz back into the father's house and have the same rights as the older brother who had never gone astray? It wasn't fair! There should be rules! There should be conditions! There should be hoops to jump through and penance to pay! After all, since the younger brother had already spent his inheritance, anything he received now would come directly from the older brother's share. Obviously, the older brother was *not* okay with that.

He wasn't okay with it because he didn't realize what he already had. Everything the father owned already belonged to the older son, but the father's joy was complete now that the younger son was home. The older brother lived his whole life in the father's house, *but he didn't have the father's heart.*

If the older brother had the father's heart, he might not have been in the house to begin with — *he might have been out looking for his brother.* Once again, Jesus is our example. He is *our* older brother. Everything the Father had was his, but he left the safety of the Father's house to seek and save the lost ones. He was willing to empty himself of his own rights and sacrificed his inheritance for our sake. *"While we still sinners, Christ died for us"* (Romans 5:8). He entered a world that had no part in him, because he knew it was the only way to bring us back to the Father. And unlike the elder brother in the parable, this elder brother did have the Father's heart.

Which example will we follow? Will we continue as the older brother in the parable—"of the world, but not in it"—and allow fear to choke out the love of the Father? Or will we follow the example of the true older brother, Jesus, and leave the safety of our comfortable surroundings to share the Father's heart for the lost ones? The choice is ours.

It's clear which choice is in the heart of the Father. Jesus said, *"As you sent me into the world, I have sent them into the world"* (John 17:18). His desire is that love will compel us beyond our fears and insecurities. His desire is that we will be willing to leave the familiar comforts and safety of home to pursue the lost and broken ones, whatever that may look like to each of us individually. *His desire is that we will share his heart.*

Everything he has is already ours; our inheritance is secure. But he doesn't yet have *his* inheritance—one pure spotless bride from every tribe, every tongue, and every nation.

The Apostle John—"the disciple Jesus loved" according to his self-description—left us with some poignant words to consider regarding the Father's heart:

> *God is love. Whoever lives in love lives in God, and God in him. In this way, love is made complete among us so that we will have confidence on the day of judgment, because in this world we are like him. There is no fear in love. But perfect love drives out fear, because fear has to do with punishment. The one who fears is not made perfect in love.*
>
> *We love because he first loved us. If anyone says, "I love God," yet hates his brother, he is a liar. For anyone who does not love his brother, whom he has seen, cannot love God, whom he has not seen. And he has given us this command: Whoever loves God must also love his brother.* **–1 John 4:16-21**

There is no fear in love. When we share the Father's heart of love, we don't need to fear the ways of the world or its influence on us. Instead, we can give ourselves with abandon to the will and desire of the Father. As we do, we will influence the world with the only power greater than the power of sin and death … *the love of God.*

III. "FOR ALL WHO WILL BELIEVE"

Hearts Beating as One

"My prayer is not for them alone. I pray also for those who will believe in me through their message, that all of them may be one, Father, just as you are in me and I am in you."–**John 17:20-21**

The final words of Jesus' prayer were for all who would believe. As he approached the cross, his eyes and his heart focused on the big picture—the joy set before him. God's ultimate goal and desire has always been for *one* Church, *one* body—and especially—for *one* bride. This is the big picture. And, astoundingly, we are invited to partner with him in realizing this desire. But what will it look like for "all of us to be one?" If this one desire is the ultimate longing of God's heart—for us to be one, as he and the Father are one—then we need to set our hearts toward understanding this great mystery from his perspective.

Lord, reveal your desires to us and help us to see each other the way you see us. Show us how to partner with you in bringing fulfillment to the ultimate longing of your heart.

CHAPTER 11

Israel, the Master Key

G woke up suddenly in the middle of the night. I wasn't alone. There was a powerful sense of God's presence in the room, manifested in a way I had not previously experienced. The weight of his glory surrounded me and permeated all of my senses. I literally couldn't move; I could scarcely breathe.

Yet I wasn't afraid. Though powerful and intense, his presence was also comforting and familiar. I laid in this state for awhile, in awe of both his glory and his grace. I didn't say a word, I'm not sure I could have if I tried. He didn't speak either—at least not at first. We simply enjoyed a time of silent fellowship, our hearts and spirits intertwined in a deep place of communion where words were not required.

It was the Lord who finally broke the silence, but I could never have anticipated his words. The Creator of the Universe himself was so close I could literally feel his breath on my cheek. In a single gentle whisper, he made an extraordinary and astounding offer:

What do you want me to do for you? I'll give you anything.

My mind reeled with possibilities. Was this for real? Did I really just hear what I thought I heard? Instinctively, I knew he wasn't asking for my prayer list. Nor was he asking what I wanted him to do for others. He wanted to do something for *me*.

These thoughts all took place in a matter of seconds. Thankfully, before I wasted much time attempting to analyze the question, my spirit responded. From somewhere deep within the core of my being, a depth of longing I didn't know existed was released. I surprised myself as I heard my own voice exclaim through enormous, gut-wrenching sobs:

"Oh, Lord! I want to go to Israel!"

His reply was immediate and simple. Just one word, actually.

Done.

And with that, the encounter was over. But my journey into understanding the depth of *his* longing for Israel had just begun.

O' Jerusalem

There is no way a book that attempts to reveal (in some fashion) the "key" to God's heart would be complete without discussing God's heart for Israel. When it comes to "unlocking" God's heart, truly Israel is the master key. The big picture will never be complete without at least a basic understanding that Israel is at the center of it all. I believe a foundational understanding of God's desire for Israel is essential for understanding his desire for *you* – and for all the nations of the earth. Without glimpsing God's heart for Israel, you will never understand the unchanging nature of his character, the depth of his commitment, and the amazing power of covenant. And you will never understand his long standing desire for *one* bride.

Although I had been praying for Israel for several years prior to that unexpected nighttime encounter, afterwards I had a far deeper desire to understand and share his heart for his chosen land and people. With the benefit of hindsight, I believe the time of silent communion I shared with the Lord had really been a time of impartation. In becoming "one" with him during those sweet moments, *his* desire for Israel was planted more deeply within my own heart. When he asked me what I wanted him to do for *me*—his desire had already become my own. A desire he fully intended to fulfill!

Not only did Jesus make a way for me to go to Israel, as he promised, but he has made a way for me to keep going and I have been many times since. The first time was indeed quite miraculous. I never told anyone about the Lord's visit that night, but God certainly didn't forget.

About a year later, the church I attended was organizing a trip to Israel. Although it seemed like the perfect opportunity to go, I was in a very tight spot financially and there was absolutely no way I could afford the trip. When I saw the notice in the church bulletin, I didn't even pray. I just sighed and said, "Well Lord, you've promised I'll go and I know *someday* I will." A few weeks later, I was sitting at my desk at work when I got a call that made my jaw drop. Despite the fact that *no one* knew about the Lord's specific promise to me, one of the pastors at the church was calling to say that an anonymous donor had had fully paid my way on the trip. Apparently God wanted to make it abundantly clear that *he keeps his promises*!

That first trip was just a beginning. Since it was a Bible study tour, we moved at a whirlwind pace in an attempt to cover as much ground as possible and we gained an amazing overview of the country. I was so incredibly grateful and blessed by the experience; the entire time I felt like Jesus was taking me home to meet the "folks." I found favorite spots around the country that endure to this day. But honestly, it was all just a little *too* fast. My heart was yearning to stay longer and linger with him in a several spots. I knew there was more he wanted to show me — especially in Jerusalem.

About two and a half years later, through a crazy rollercoaster ride of events, I had the opportunity to return. I knew it would be a *very* different trip. I was going for nearly a month and I was staying primarily in Jerusalem. For the first ten days or so, I participated in a large international conference celebrating the Feast of Tabernacles. After that, I had the opportunity to stay for a couple of additional weeks with an acquaintance who lived in the heart of Jerusalem. Before leaving I told the Lord that I had seen Israel through the eyes of the tour guides, this time I wanted to see Israel through *his* eyes.

Almost as soon as I got off the plane, things *were* different. Although the Lord was doing a lot in me personally when I made the first trip, the trip itself was very easy. For the most part everything went smoothly and everyone had a great time. This time, everything did *not* go smoothly. It would take way too many words to try to explain all that took place, but suffice it to say I have never experienced such an intense level of spiritual warfare in my life. It seemed that the very legions of hell were conspiring on every side to chase me out of the country with my head down and my tail between my legs — if not worse. It was difficult and it was exhausting. But it also didn't work.

Instead, I leaned into Jesus and fell in love with him all over again. I fell in love with him *and* with the nation and in his people he has forever claimed as his own. I tasted something heart much deeper than anything I had known to that point. His depth of longing for – and commitment to – the people and land of Israel caught me completely off guard. He literally broke my heart as he shared *his* heart with me. This was especially true while I was in the city of Jerusalem.

It seemed that every single time I looked out over the city, I would start weeping. I couldn't help but think of Jesus as he sat on the Mount of Olives and wept as he looked out over his beloved city. One evening during this time, I wrote the following words:

> *Looking out over the city tonight, his tears fill my eyes. Sitting on my balcony in the newer part of Jerusalem, my physical eyes are taking in a sight that would seem commonplace in any one of thousands of cities around the globe. But this isn't just any city – this is his city. This is Jerusalem. Jerusalem, the apple of his eye. Jerusalem, who kills the prophets and stones those sent to her. Jerusalem, the city whose children Jesus longs to gather as a hen gathers her chicks under her wings. Jerusalem, the one and only place God Almighty has chosen to establish his eternal throne. Jerusalem, the holy city of God.*
>
> *I can't make sense of it. I refuse to even try. Trying to understand the heart of God with human reasoning is about as absurd as a two-year-old trying to fully comprehend the cosmos. You don't comprehend the heart of God, you feel the heart of God. As I sit with him tonight, I have an overwhelming sense that he doesn't want me to dissect his emotions so that I might be able to rationalize them in some nice tidy way – he simply wants me to share them. So together we watch the city. And together we cry.*

Yes, he still weeps, he still waits, and he still watches. Like a forsaken Lover, like a forgiving Father – he weeps, he waits, and he watches. He continues to extend his arm in compassion and mercy. He continues to reach out with his offer of love, forgiveness, and true peace. And, for the most part, she continues to rebel against him and reject his love. His heart breaks – so he weeps, he waits, and he watches.

*It's tempting to make some analogy about how he watches and waits for us, too. It's tempting to say that we are not so different from Jerusalem in how we often rebel against him and reject his love. It's tempting – but it's not entirely true. While he most certainly does watch and wait for **all** of his wayward children, and while many around the globe most certainly do rebel against him and reject his love – Jerusalem is different. Only Jerusalem is Jerusalem. Like it or not, understand it or not – only Jerusalem is Jerusalem. The Church is not Israel; Israel is Israel. And Israel – even more specifically Jerusalem – holds an eternal place in the heart of God reserved for no other. So he weeps, he waits, and he watches.*

I don't fully understand it. I don't need to. Tonight I'm content to simply watch and wait with him. As I do, for just a moment, I see him smile through his tears.

Yes, only Jerusalem is Jerusalem. And God's faithfulness to this eternal city – and to the entire nation of Israel – will endure forever.

God's Unconditional Love and Irrevocable Calling

Although I have certainly tasted the love in God's heart for Israel, I do not profess to be an expert when it comes to the Lord's plans and purposes for this nation and its people. The political, social, and spiritual dynamics in Israel are among the most intense and complex on the planet. There is always much going on, much to take in, and many differing opinions. It's easy to get caught up in the overload. Many sincere believers genuinely sense God tugging on their heartstrings to pray for, and stand with, Israel, but they end up confused or discouraged because of all the religious and political posturing surrounding this tiny nation. There is a vast amount of division and disagreement concerning Israel even within the Church. In politics, in preaching, and often even in prayer, when it comes to Israel there are no lack of voices clamoring to be heard!

When people ask about my own trips to Israel I have often struggled to find the right words to express why I go and what it is I'm trying to do while there. I think I've complicated things by trying to meet what I assume to be others' expectations. The simple truth is that I go because I believe God—I believe he is who he said he is, and that he will do what he says he will do. I believe he is the God of Abraham, Isaac and Jacob, and that he *will* fulfill his plans and purposes for his covenant people and his covenant land. Even more, I go simply because I love Jesus and the more intimately I have come to know his heart, the more I have come to love what he loves. He loves Israel—and so do I. No politics. No agenda. Just simple faith that says "yes" to the desires of God's heart.

Having said that, I also desire to have a solid foundation of biblical understanding for the things God has so deeply imprinted on my heart by his Spirit. There are many "interesting" ideas concerning Israel that the Church has embraced in part or in full over the years. Of these ideas, one of the most prevalent is "replacement theology." In a nutshell, replacement theology asserts that due to Israel's rejection of Jesus as the Messiah, the Church has now "replaced" Israel in God's plans—and in his affections. According to this school of

126

thought, all of the promises made to Israel now apply to the Church instead.

A slightly different twist on this position that has gained steam in recent years asserts that Jesus has now *fulfilled* God's plans for Israel. It is absolutely true that Jesus *did* fulfill the law and prophets (see Matt. 5:17), but God's covenant with Abraham (which includes the land) *preceded* the law and the prophets. God's covenant with Abraham was (and is) unconditional and irrevocable.

Can many of the promises and prophecies made concerning Israel be applied in a broader sense to the Church? Of course, but that certainly doesn't mean they no longer apply in their original context to natural Israel and to the natural sons (and daughters) of Abraham. And yes, many prophecies were fulfilled in Jesus and others find a more complete fulfillment when applied to all of God's people, but a progressive layer of truth revealed in God's promises does not make the initial intent of the promises null and void.

Think of it, if God were to turn his back on Israel and decide they have now been "replaced" in his heart and purposes because they failed to respond appropriately, how can we possibly trust him to remain faithful to his promises in *our* lives? As the Apostle Paul exclaims, *"Did God reject his people? By no means!"* (Romans 11:1). Most of us have no trouble claiming the promise in Romans 11:29 for ourselves — *"For God's gifts and his call are irrevocable"* — but the context of this new covenant passage refers to the irrevocable nature of God's gifts and call *to Israel*. He hasn't changed his mind about me, he hasn't changed his mind about you — and he *certainly* hasn't changed his mind about Israel!

On the flip side of this issue, there is another extremely unfortunate and dangerous doctrine being promoted by some who consider themselves sincere friends of Israel and the Jewish people. It is most commonly referred to as "dual covenant theology" and asserts that since Jews already have a special covenantal relationship with God, they do not need to recognize and accept Jesus as their Messiah to access heaven. Yet Jesus himself said, *"I am the way and the truth and the life. No one comes to the Father except through me"* (John 14:6). All of the early believers were, in fact, Jewish and they seemed to think it was imperative to share the good news of Jesus' death, burial and resurrection with their fellow Jews! Simply entertaining the possibility that somehow the Jewish people have another means of salvation, not only makes a mockery of Jesus' "once for all" sacrifice but also hinders our fervency to share the gospel and pray for the salvation of the Jewish people. And for the One who still watches and waits for the lost sheep of Israel to come home—nothing could break his heart more.

It is far beyond the scope of this book to provide a more detailed look into any of these issues. I have included these few paragraphs on some of the more prevalent areas of distortion and disagreement concerning Israel, simply to raise an awareness of their existence and, hopefully, stir your heart to learn more. But, as always, I am far more interested in stirring a desire to press into God's heart—so you can hear what he has to say about Israel for yourself.

One New Man—and One Bride

Again, I freely confess that I do not fully understand all the nuances of the various theological positions concerning Israel. But I don't need to. When faced with an overload of information I don't understand, I have learned to dial things down to their simplest essence and hold fast to what I know to be true. And there are indeed several things revealed in the

Scriptures that I do know to be true concerning God's heart and desire specifically for Israel.

"There is neither Jew nor Gentile, neither slave nor free, nor is there male and female, for you are all one in Christ Jesus" (Gal. 3:28). We **are** all *one* in Christ. There is neither Jew nor Gentile *in* Christ—yet there *is* a distinction between Jew and Gentile that is as significant as the distinction between being male or female. The early Church experienced a huge paradigm shift when God clearly revealed that his offer of salvation was available to both Jew *and* Gentile. There were many believing Jews who felt Gentiles needed to observe the law in order to be saved. As the Church age has progressed, this idea has flipped and many in the Church now believe that any Jew who comes to accept Jesus as their Messiah must conform to our western ideas of church and lose their "Jewish-ness" since they are no longer required to observe the law. Neither position is wholly correct. We *are* one in Christ, but we also have separate and distinct heritages and roles in God's plan of salvation to the nations.

The Apostle Paul, an Israelite himself, carried a keen understanding of God's heart and desire for Israel. In Romans 11:11, he asks (concerning Israel), *"Did they stumble so as to fall beyond recovery? Not at all! Rather, because of their transgression, salvation has come to the Gentiles to make Israel envious."* Church, *this* is our role. God desires that we live the reality of "Christ in us" to such a degree that we provoke Israel to jealousy and, as a result, open her blind eyes to the goodness and grace of her own Messiah.

There are many schools of thought and eschatological (end times) positions regarding God's dealings with Israel, but since the Bible says, *"Now is the day of salvation"* (2 Corinthians 6:2), I would suggest you have reason to question *any* position that implies God will not draw or save the Jewish people until other events have first taken place. I whole-heartedly agree that we should be students of the Word and aware of the times and seasons in which we live, but an out-of-balance focus on the unfolding of end-time events can draw our attention away from what God is doing right in front of us. While we always need to be awake and alert, our focus should be on knowing and rightly representing the heart of our beautiful Bridegroom King—*here and now*—so that others (both Jew and Gentile) are continually drawn to him.

> *But now in Christ Jesus you who once were far away have been brought near through the blood of Christ. For he himself is our peace, who has made the two one and has destroyed the barrier, the dividing wall of hostility, by abolishing in his flesh the law with its commandments and regulations. His purpose was to create in himself **one new man** out of the two (Jew and Gentile), thus making peace, and in this one body to reconcile both of them to God through the cross, by which he put to death their hostility.*
> *–Ephesians 2:3-16*

Together in Christ we are one new man. Together in Christ we are one body. And together in Christ we will come together as his one long-awaited bride. *"But if their (Israel's) transgression means riches for the world, and their loss means riches for the Gentiles, how much greater riches will their fullness bring!"* (Romans 11:12). How I long for the fullness the salvation of Israel will bring to the body of Messiah! Even more, how I long for the fullness of joy the salvation of Israel will bring to God's heart!

God *will* remain forever faithful to his first-born nation and people. And if we want to partner with him in his heart and desires, we must remain faithful to Israel as well. The Church has, and forever will have, Jewish roots. Eternally, we will worship a Jewish King. Esther tried to hide her Jewish roots, but when push came to shove and the fate of her entire race was on the line, Esther finally revealed her heritage and stood in the gap for her people (Esther 4).

What about us? There are "spiritual forces of evil" at work that would like to wipe Israel off the face of the Earth. It is these same forces that attempt to confuse, silence, and divide the Church. A day is coming when those in the Church will no longer have the luxury of neutrality and we will need to choose whether or not we are willing to openly reveal our Jewish roots. I know where I stand, but what about you? *"Who knows whether you have come to the kingdom for such a time as this?"* (Esther 4:14 NKJV). We *need* each other. We need to stand for, and with, each other. Because only together—Jew and Gentile—will Jesus' longing for *one* pure spotless bride finally be realized.

CHAPTER 12

The Big Picture

Jesus was standing before me in a tuxedo. It was clear that he was ready for the wedding, but he was still waiting for his bride. As I stood watching him, he did something shocking. In one swift movement, he brought those beautiful nail-scarred hands up to his chest and then—reminiscent of Clark Kent tearing into his shirt to reveal the blazing "S" of Superman hidden beneath his business suit—he tore not only through the front of his tuxedo and shirt, but also right through the wall of his chest. He literally opened and exposed his heart. As the blood streamed out of his open heart, it flowed into a red carpet. I realized immediately that he was extending an invitation. He stood there and watched—waiting patiently for his bride to respond.

This invitation went beyond coming to him for salvation—*this was an invitation into his very heart.* This was an invitation to be one with him. An invitation to live and move and breathe *in* him. This was an invitation into a place of communion so deep that nothing would ever look the same again.

The Lord allowed me to witness this scene as an observer — watching and waiting along with him. After waiting for what seemed like a very long time, finally, one brave soul accepted the invitation and started on the journey toward his heart. Soon another followed. Then another. And another. Although I was happy some were beginning to respond, I was sad there weren't more. Many watched with curiosity, but only a few said "yes."

I continued watching as various individuals here and there accepted his invitation and began the journey into the deep places of his heart. Then something unexpected happened. A small group of people — five in all — linked arms. With great purpose and determination etched on their faces, they walked toward his heart together. As they did, the Lord responded in a way that is burned into my heart and memory to this day. He took a deep breath, closed his eyes as he tilted his head heavenward, then let out the most euphoric and contented sigh I have ever heard. In fact, I didn't just hear it — *I felt it*. That single united action, by a very small group of people, brought a level of pleasure and satisfaction to his heart that I have never tapped into before or since.

A Corporate Invitation

Every time I think of his response, it brings tears to my eyes — and a determination to my heart. *I want him to have what he desires.* He is after something so much deeper, so much bigger, and so much more profound than anything we can imagine. Yet he wants us to imagine it with him. He wants us to partner with him. He wants *us* — individually and corporately — to share the longings of his heart.

It *is* hard to imagine, let alone communicate, what sharing his heart on a corporate level will look like. I simply don't know. I don't know what it will look like, I don't know what it will feel like, and I don't know how to get there—*but I want to find out*. I want to find out because I know it's what *he* wants. I hope you want to find out too. Like Joshua and the Israelites as they prepared to cross the Jordan, our only option on this journey is to follow "the ark" (his presence) because "*we have never been this way before*" (Joshua 3:4).

As a whole, the Body of Christ is greater than the sum of its parts. "*In Christ we who are many form one body, and each member belongs to all the others*" (Romans 12:5). While God created us in distinctly unique ways, we are only complete together. Some of the most profound times of worship I've ever experienced have been times of intimate, solitary communion with Jesus. I treasure those times and will *always* spend time seeking him alone in the secret place, but in recent years there has been an increased longing deep within my soul to experience a much greater *corporate* reality.

When we unite our hearts together in worship, each of us brings our own history with Jesus into our group gatherings. The greater the diversity in our unique experiences, personalities, gifts, and expressions of worship, the more broadly and accurately we reflect his vast creative nature. Think of the different scenes of worship painted throughout the book of Revelation—the saints and elders, angels of all kinds, the living creatures—all so different, *yet perfectly united in worship*. Each unique, yet complimenting each other and together bringing a far more complete expression of worship than could ever be possible individually. If this is heaven's model and we pray as Jesus taught us, "*On earth as it is in heaven*" then what should our corporate worship look like here and now?

Brian Johnson has a song called "What Does it Sound Like?" The lyrics are simple:

What does it sound like when we sing heaven's songs?

What does it feel like when heaven comes down?

What does it look like when God is all around?

Let it come.

Each time I hear the song, my spirit is stirred in a deep way. What *will* it sound like when we sing heaven's songs? When we join the saints and angels gathered around the throne? When we are united in love and truly sing with one heart, one mind, and one accord? When there is no possibility of distraction because all our energy, all our focus, and all our affection is steadfastly fixed upon the One seated on the throne?

What *will* it feel like when heaven comes down? When "Thy kingdom come, thy will be done, on earth as it is in heaven" is an overwhelming present-tense reality rather than a tagline to our prayers? When the not yet becomes the now? When heaven so invades this earth that the two become one?

What *will* it look like when God is all around? When his manifest presence is a shared reality so profound that it is no longer a personal experience open to subjective interpretation? When all of our senses and all of our emotions are consumed by the light of his glory? When our eyes behold the unfathomable beauty of the Bridegroom King?

What will it sound like? What will it feel like? What will it look like? *I don't know.* I don't think any of us do … yet.

I've had glimpses. I've had tastes. Maybe you have too. But I want more. I want to *know* what it sounds like with my physical ears. I want to *know* what it feels like with all of my senses. I want to *know* what it looks like with my physical eyes. And I want to share it with you—right here and right now. What's more, I'm convinced this is Jesus' desire too.

The fullness won't come until he does, but until then I long to know just as much as it *is* possible to know. I want to be amongst those willing to link arms and journey into uncharted territories. *I want to see his longing fulfilled.* I want to hear that sigh again, not just in a vision, but in real time as his people respond in one accord and say "yes" to his invitation.

Reflecting His Glory

Several earlier chapters of this book focused on apprehending the personal knowledge that God is madly, passionately, head-over-heels in love with *you*—and he is! But this knowledge should stir within us a greater desire to love and know *him*. Knowing him should stir a greater desire to love what he loves. It's ironic that we will never truly understand God's heart, until we know, on a heart level, how deeply and intimately involved he is with each of us individually. But once we *do* begin grasp this fact, it should begin to change—*and broaden*—our focus.

Although God does know and love each of us individually and personally, he is after more. He is after the collective us, not just the individual us. Each of us uniquely represents a facet of his character in a way no one else can. We are each essential to the whole. When we fail to take our unique place in the body, we deny the world that specific glimpse of his face. Each facet is wonderful, but it is only together that we rightly reflect the beauty of his countenance and the fullness of his glory.

God told Abraham that his descendants would be *"as numerous as the stars in the sky"* (Gen. 26:4). Isaiah tells us that God *"brings out the starry host one by one, and calls them each by* name. Because of his great power and mighty strength, not one of them is missing" (Isaiah 40:2). Each star is an amazing and awe-inspiring creation all on its own. When you consider that our sun, the closest star to earth, is just an average star, you have some idea of each star's individual beauty and brilliance. God knows each one by name — not one is missing. Individually they are unique and brilliant, yet it is their beauty and function *together* that makes up the universe. Can you imagine looking up into the night sky and seeing only a few lone stars?

Individually we have great beauty and purpose — brilliance even — yet we only recognize the fullness of our purpose as part of the whole. When we step back and look at the dazzling splendor of all he has created, we recognize just how small we each are individually. Despite this fact, *he* knows each of us by name and we are never out of his sight. It is amazing to think we are such a tiny part, and yet such a huge part, of God's plan all at the same time! Though we each represent only a very small part of the whole, each and every part is unique, valuable, and *vital*.

We may shine individually, but we light up the darkness together. When several burning embers are pushed together, they create a great flame. Apart they merely burn out. We really are better together — and it is only together that we give the world an authentic glimpse of his glory.

"When I consider your heavens, the work of your fingers, the moon and the stars, which you have set in place, what is man that you are mindful of him, the son of man that you care for him?" (Psalm 8:3-4). These verses point to the stunning reality that he *is* mindful of me. He *is* mindful of you. But even more — he is mindful of *us*. When I consider the unfathomable vastness of who he is and what he has created, it is astounding to recognize the Lord has such a deep and intimate interest in each of one of us. But when considering the immensity of the

universe and the majesty of his Being, it is also incredibly obvious — *this whole thing is not about me.*

Getting a Glimpse

The phrase "it's not about me" has become a bit of a Christian cliché in recent years. Is it true? Oh yeah! In ways that are, I suspect, far beyond our current understanding. But it shouldn't be something we say; it should be a truth we live. We don't live it by reciting it until we convince ourselves of its reality — *we live it by glimpsing the big picture.*

As Misty Edwards has often sung from the prayer room at the International House of Prayer in Kansas City: *"There's something bigger going on, there's Someone bigger than me."* That "Someone" has a dream in his heart, and it's *his* dream that is at the heart of the big picture.

When I look back over the last five or six years, I realize the Lord unraveled and rewired the way I look at just about everything — especially spiritual things. Looking back with the benefit of hindsight, I can see that he pulled back the curtain — for just a moment — and I glimpsed the big picture in a way I never had before. For me, it changed *everything.*

I have always been blessed with spiritual hunger and I have longed for Jesus deeply and often through the years. But starting with the encounter that served as the catalyst for this manuscript and culminating with my second trip to Israel (described in the previous chapter), my definition of longing and depth — and a whole lot of other things — began to change dramatically. What I once thought to be "deep," now seemed like dipping my toes into a child's wading pool. As for longing, well, let's just say I didn't even begin to understand what longing was — *until I tasted his.*

It was an interesting season to navigate. For a long time, I felt like I was in a free-fall. All the old props—the spiritual clichés, the black and white boxes of my doctrine and beliefs, the things I thought I knew, what I thought I was called to do and be, the comforts of structure and familiarity—were kicked out from underneath me. I felt like I had to unlearn and then relearn almost everything. Frankly, I'm still not done unlearning and relearning! I don't think I ever will be.

Despite all the changes, far and away the most challenging and painful thing to cope with during this season was the unceasing ache in my heart. For about a year, I ached for Jesus with an intensity that was nearly unbearable. It started right before that life changing second trip to Israel and intensified afterwards. My heart began to yearn for his presence so desperately that I literally couldn't bear to be away from him. Each day, I felt as though my heart was breaking into a million pieces—each piece longing to find its home in him. I feared that I had gone too far—gotten out of balance—didn't keep healthy boundaries—taken a wrong turn somewhere. Something along those lines seemed to make the most sense. But the things of his heart rarely make sense to our human understanding. When I stopped to listen, I heard his Spirit say something very different:

He reminded me that I *asked* for this.

And I had. I asked for his heart. In fact, I *pleaded* with him to share his heart with me. I said I didn't care what it cost. I said I didn't care how desperately it caused me to ache for him. I told him I *had* to taste the deep places of his heart. Apparently he believed me, because he answered.

He let me taste. But in his mercy, it was *just* a taste. At that point, I truly don't believe I could have taken any more. As he reminded me of my prayers—my pleas, really—the veil lifted and for the first time I understood. I mean, I didn't just say I understood, *I really understood.* The pain, the ache, the all-consuming passion, the jealous zeal, the longing to deep for words, the desperate desire that seemed as though it would completely consume me — *it wasn't even mine.*

It was his.

It has always been, and until it reaches its ultimate fulfillment, it will always be, *his.* My ache was the echo; his was, and is, the Source.

I always knew Jesus longed for his bride, but in the shallowness of my humanity, I really didn't get it. Although he does long for me — passionately — *he has me.* He doesn't have his bride. And *his* heart's desire will never be fulfilled until she is with him where he is — *forever.*

Until that time, he invites *us* to share his longing. He invites *us* to watch and wait with him. He invites *us* to come closer; to draw nearer. He invites us into the mysteries of his heart. "*My prayer is not for them alone. I pray also for those who will believe in me through their message*" (John 17:20). His invitation is never to just a few. It's to all who will believe.

The invitation has been extended. It's good to say "yes" individually — and we need to do that first — but it's better together. This is so much deeper than his longing for any individual. It is deeper, even, than his longing for a people group or nation. It's his longing for the collective us — for *one* pure spotless bride.

In many ways, this *is* uncharted territory. There is no map or simple list of instructions, but there *is* a red carpet. And there *is* an Escort — the Holy Spirit. It's *his* desire that we say "yes." When we do, his presence will go with us. *But that doesn't mean it will be easy.* There *is* such a thing as tasting too much, seeing too much, feeling too much, knowing too much, to ever turn back. Once you've experienced the ocean, the safe waters of the wading pool forever lose their appeal. Expect the unexpected. Expect to be undone. Expect to be ruined.

It requires courage to leave the familiar and head into the unknown. It requires trust—in him *and* in each other. But if the Creator of the Universe has chosen to trust frail, fickle humans with the very depths of his heart, the very least we can do is trust him with ours.

When we do, I can't wait to look up and see the smile on his face. Even more, I can't wait to once again hear that deep, contented sigh of satisfaction. Most of all, I can't wait for him to have what he desires.

Oh Lord —*please* — let it come!

CHAPTER 13

That All of Them May Be One

*I*n the spirit, I saw a coin spinning on its axis. As I watched it spin and spin and spin, I heard the Holy Spirit whispering to my heart:

Two sides; same coin.

I had been seeking the Lord for understanding. I was confused. It seemed like every time I turned around, men and women of God — sincere lovers of Jesus whom I greatly loved and respected — were contradicting each other with their views. Issues that had once seemed black and white were suddenly cloaked in gray. I wanted truth! One would speak with passion and authority on a particular issue and there would be a powerful witness of the Spirit on the words spoken. Then another would speak — *with a diametrically opposed view of the very same issue* — and again there would be a powerful witness of the Spirit.

How was this possible? God never contradicts himself — right?

Two sides, same coin.

Or put another way, *one* body with many members. And we *don't* all function the same way.

Embracing the Paradox

This became my answer. While it is absolutely true that God never contradicts himself and he never contradicts his Word, it is also true that *our* current understanding of his ways and of his Word are woefully lacking. God never contradicts himself, but he definitely (and frequently) contradicts our *current limited understanding.*

I love the song by Kate Miner, "Jesus, You are Holy." There is a line in that song that always struck a chord with me, but in recent years it has become lodged in my heart and spirit at a much deeper level: *Joy and sorrow, deeply mingled. Yes! The glory of the cross!*

Joy *and* sorrow. Polar opposites, yet both real. Both *true.* Both existing at the same time. Neither higher nor more true than the other. This simple line perfectly illustrates a concept that I have come to believe that we, the global Church of Jesus Christ, *must* apprehend if we are ever to walk in true unity of heart, mind, and spirit. We must embrace the mystery of the paradox (briefly discussed in Chapter 5) — the strange reality that truth is often held in the tension that exists between precepts that appear, at least on the surface, to contradict each other. There are concepts that contradict each other in *our* finite minds and finite world, *but those same concepts exist without contradiction in God's infinite kingdom.*

If we're honest, most of us are pretty attached to our opinions and to our pet doctrines. We tend to think the things *we* are most passionate about are the things that are most important. We like to think the truths we have personally apprehended are the superior truths. What we're learning, everyone should be learning. If we've received breakthrough in a certain area by doing "a,b,c" then everyone should do that and they will have breakthrough too! Well, *maybe*. But then again — maybe not.

Some people have tapped into the joy of heaven and are great cheerleaders who love to rejoice with those who rejoice. But weeping with those who weep? Not so much. After all, shouldn't everyone just be thankful for what they have and be positive? Why are some people so heavy-hearted when God is so good? Others are filled with deep compassion and gladly come alongside to comfort and weep with those who are brokenhearted and suffering. But those same people often look upon those with light, merry hearts as being shallow and insensitive. How can you rejoice when so many people are hurting? Which is true?

On and on it goes. Many focus on apprehending the power of the resurrection that is ours in Christ; others seek to know the deep intimacy of sharing in his suffering. Some have tapped into the amazing freedom of living under grace; others willingly give themselves as bond-slaves for the sake of others. I know many whose mandate is to see the reality of the atonement manifested in the healing of sick and broken human bodies; I know many others who believe that healing of the heart and soul is of greater importance. Many contend for the "suddenly's" of God — divine encounters that bring change in an instant; others believe that quiet perseverance in tried and true disciplines of faith is the only sure way of staying the course.

Entire movements place preeminence upon study of the written Word of God; other movements upon the power and presence of the Holy Spirit. Some see his kingdom coming "on earth as it is in heaven" in ever increasing measure; others have a fervent urgency to prepare the Church for the darkness coming upon the earth. Some feel called to "be" — other called to "do." Some fervently and persistently ask, seek, and knock and are the "violent who take the kingdom by force;" others rest and wait patiently for the Lord. And let's not forget that granddaddy paradox of them all: Those who passionately believe God exercises absolute sovereign control over every detail of life on the planet; and those who just as passionately believe in the right and responsibility of man to choose his own path.

These are deep and complex issues that have been debated by brilliant minds throughout the ages. Of course, each of these "sides" reveal a facet of the truth, but truth is only complete when considered in the whole. And, once again, only God sees the whole picture. Anyone who believes they have simple pat answers that tie all these concepts together with a nice neat bow, or conversely, anyone who believes there is a version of truth that holds to some of these precepts and discards others, has not honestly and thoughtfully considered the issues. To complicate things further, some of us will relate more to different sides of the coin in different seasons of life, but just because *we* change seasons, doesn't mean everyone we know changes along with us! Sometimes we *won't* be on the same page with everyone else, but that does not necessarily mean someone is on the wrong page. *It simply means we're different.* Our finite minds have trouble with that concept. We want things to be either right or wrong. Sometimes they are either one or the other — but often they are not.

We will never understand it all. And because we don't, our attitude toward those with opinions, experiences, passions, and callings different from our own, should consistently be one of love and grace. Does that mean I'm saying everything is relative and there is no such thing as absolute truth? It should be clear from previous chapters of this book that I am not implying that at all. What I *am* saying is that our current understanding of truth is always limited. We want to boil truth down to mere precepts. But Jesus himself will always be *the* Truth—and he is much more than a set of precepts.

Only Jesus walked the paradox perfectly. He told us to enter by the narrow gate and I am convinced that truth held in tension *is* the narrow gate. We tend to think our black and white ideals represent the narrow path, but in reality that is a very broad road that has led to much destruction and division within the body of Christ. *"But small is the gate and narrow the road that leads to life and there are only a few who find it"* (Matt. 7:14). The key to that gate is humility and love.

We don't all start at the same place. We don't all have the same advantages and disadvantages. We don't have the same temperaments and passions. We don't all live in the same culture and we didn't grow up in the same environment. We don't have the same abilities, the same gifts, or the same calling. *So how on earth can we possibly expect faith and faithfulness to look the same on each of us?*

Holy Ground

With all of my heart I believe we are on the verge of a new day. We are on the verge of taking new spiritual territory in this strange area of unity. It's a big, big deal. An army that is united cannot be stopped. When the Israelites were getting ready to face the walled city of Jericho (Joshua 5:13-15)—a situation that seemed impossible and impassible—Joshua looked toward the city and encountered "the Angel of the Lord" (a pre-incarnate appearance of Jesus). His question sounds awfully familiar:

"Are you for us, or for our enemies?"

But what was the Lord's response?

"No!" (Some translations say "Neither!")

In other words—*wrong question Josh!* When we ask the wrong questions, we tend to get some pretty perplexing responses from the Lord. But I think Joshua got it a lot faster than many of us do, because he quickly and wisely fell on his face and asked a much better question:

"What message does my Lord have for his servant?"

The Commander of the Lord's army replied "Take off your sandals for the place you are standing is holy."

The place you are standing is holy. Think about that. Let it sink in. In Christ we stand. The place *we* stand is holy. The place we abide, the place we dwell—is holy.

Beloved, we are on holy ground. *That* is the issue and not what side of the coin we are on in any given conflict within the Church. So often we are wasting time and energy asking the wrong questions, when Jesus himself is standing right before us ready to lead us into new territory. What message does he have for *us?* What is he saying, what is he doing—*right now?* Better yet, how can we join him? These are the questions we should be asking.

After Jesus' resurrection you may recall he had a little unfinished business with a particularly exuberant disciple named Peter (John 21:15-23). Jesus was talking to Peter about the plans he had for him, but instead of giving the Lord his full attention Peter was distracted by some things he'd heard about John. The things he heard didn't make sense to him. Jesus knew what Peter was thinking and cut right to the chase: *"If I want him to remain alive until I return, what is that to you? You must follow me."*

You notice Jesus didn't bother to clarify Peter's misperceptions, he just told Peter to follow him. That's what I need to do. That's what you need to do. That's what *we* need to do—*follow him.*

Jesus is the Head over the Church and over the body. When each of us is rightly related to the Head, then we will each perform *our* right function. My function may be completely different than yours; in fact, our functions (and perspectives) *need* to be different if we ever hope for the body to be whole.

One Accord

Often, I suspect we are moving in greater harmony of mind and heart than we realize. Due to our diversity, our outward expressions of a united desire to love and please God may look very different. As a result, we assume we are more divided than we are in reality. However, when left uncorrected these false assumptions lead to actions that *do* cause division and destruction.

The eastern tribes of Israel (the Reubenites, the Gadites and the half-tribe of Manasseh) learned something about being the victims of false assumptions (See Joshua 22). After the Promised Land had been taken, these tribes were finally allowed to return to their own homes on the eastern side of the Jordan. When they returned, they built an altar as a witness between them and the other tribes so all future generations would know they were united in their worship of the one true God. Unfortunately, their sincere act of worship was misunderstood. Since the other tribes didn't have a paradigm for an altar of this nature, they *assumed* the altar was built as an act of rebellion and idolatry:

When they came to Geliloth near the Jordan in the land of Canaan, the Reubenites, the Gadites and the half-tribe of Manasseh built an imposing altar there by the Jordan. And when the Israelites heard that they had built the altar on the border of Canaan at Geliloth near the Jordan on the Israelite side, the whole assembly of Israel gathered at Shiloh to go to war against them. **–Joshua 22:10-12**

When their own brothers heard about what the eastern tribes had done—*before they bothered to check it out for themselves*—they gathered to go to war against them. Hmm, that sounds a little too close for comfort. How many times have *you* heard someone criticizing another church or ministry, essentially declaring war over them with words, without any first-hand information of what that church or ministry actually stands for?

Fortunately, before actually physically advancing against them, they confronted them: *"How could you break faith with the God of Israel like this? How could you turn away from the Lord and build yourselves an altar in rebellion against him now"* (Joshua 22:16).

The Israelites *assumed* their eastern brothers were rebelling against the Lord because what they built didn't look like any previous example they had of authentic worship to the living God. It's interesting that even in Israel's confrontation of the situation they seemed to be motivated more out of fear for their own necks than out of genuine devotion to the Lord or concern for the eastern tribes:

"If you rebel against the LORD today, tomorrow he will be angry with the whole community of Israel. If the land you possess is defiled, come over to the LORD's land, where the LORD's tabernacle stands, and share the land with us. But

do not rebel against the LORD or against us by building an altar for yourselves, other than the altar of the LORD our God. When Achan son of Zerah was unfaithful in regard to the devoted things, did not wrath come on the whole community of Israel? He was not the only one who died for his sin." –**Joshua 22:18-20**

Their assumption was that the eastern tribes had built the altar for themselves; their fear was that God would judge the *whole* of Israel for this "rebellious" action; and their solution was that the eastern tribes should come over to "their side" in order to truly worship the Lord. They were wrong on all three counts.

The eastern tribes wisely entrusted themselves into the Lord's hands:

"If we have built our own altar to turn away from the LORD and to offer burnt offerings and grain offerings, or to sacrifice fellowship offerings on it, may the LORD himself call us to account. No! We did it for fear that some day your descendants might say to ours, 'What do you have to do with the LORD, the God of Israel? The LORD has made the Jordan a boundary between us and you — you Reubenites and Gadites! You have no share in the LORD.' So your descendants might cause ours to stop fearing the LORD." –Joshua 22:23-24

The very thing Israel feared had been built to turn the eastern tribes away from the God of Israel, had, in fact, been built by a group of forward thinkers desiring to *bridge* any gap that may arise in future generations. The action of the eastern tribes was not only intended to honor God — it was also intended to *unite* them with their brothers on the other side of the Jordan for years to come. The Israelites quickly jumped to the wrong conclusion regarding the eastern tribes, because they filtered it through their own past experiences and didn't have a paradigm for that particular expression of devotion.

How often do we do the same? How many sincere acts of unity and worship have we misinterpreted as acts of rebellion and idolatry? How often have those with a different perspective and place in the body, reached out to other parts of the body with an olive branch, only to be met with suspicion and mistrust? How often have the pioneers and forerunners — those who see a little farther ahead than most of the body — been accused of stepping outside the boundaries of what's currently understood as safe and acceptable?

What if, instead of suspicion and mistrust, our first response was love? John Wesley once said, "Though we cannot think alike, may we not love alike? May we not be of one heart, though we are not of one opinion? Without all doubt, we may. Herein all the children of God may unite, notwithstanding these smaller differences."

According to the Apostle Paul in 1 Corinthians 13:7, love *"always protects, always trusts, always hopes, always perseveres."* God *is* love. If we are rightly related to the Head — and filled with *his* love — it is much easier to trust *each other.* There would be far greater unity in the body if we simply trusted each other to be in sincere partnership with the Holy Spirit, even when the results of that partnership look very different from one person, or even one movement, to the next.

The early Church in the book of Acts may be the best example we have to date of a healthy, united Church:

"Every day they continued to meet together (many translations say they "continued in one accord") *in the temple courts. They broke bread in their homes and ate*

together with glad and sincere hearts, praising God and enjoying the favor of all the people. And the Lord added to their number daily those who were being saved." –**Acts 2:46-47**

Yet even in the early days of the Church—which was a fraction of the size of the current Church—there were many issues that caused sharp disagreement and division. For a time, despite the areas of disagreement, the Church continued in "one accord." However it is clear from the later writings of Paul and from Church history that this did not continue. What changed?

Could it be that they, like us, lost their focus on the Source of unity? When Jesus prayed *"that they may be one"* he also added, *"as we* (Jesus and the Father) *are one"*(John 17:11). It is important to remember that our model for unity is the unity between the Father, Son, and Holy Spirit—and not a pattern of *conformity* to a particular set of doctrinal thoughts or ideals. There is further revelation of this concept in the book of Ephesians, *"Make every to **keep** the unity of the Spirit through the bond of peace"* (Eph. 4:3). The clear implication is that since we all have the same Spirit, we need only *maintain*, rather than *attain*, the unity we already have in the Spirit.

Recognizing all sincere believers in the Lordship of Jesus as true brothers and sisters, without name calling and finger-pointing in the areas where we disagree, is the first step in keeping the unity of the Spirit, *"Until we all reach unity in the faith and in the knowledge of the Son of God and become mature, attaining to the whole measure of the fullness of Christ"* (Eph. 4:13).

Church, it is time to grow up. It is time to grow *"in the knowledge of the Son of God and become mature."* Maybe if we set our hearts on simply following as he leads; maybe if we fall on our faces and ask the right questions instead of the wrong ones;

maybe if our eyes are fixed on that glorious Man who stands in front of us ready to lead us in triumph; then maybe—just maybe—instead of seeing two sides, we will finally begin to see *one coin*. Then maybe we will begin to see *one* Church and *one* body. Then maybe we will begin to understand what it really means to be *one with him*. Then maybe we will begin to care more about *his* desire for one bride, than our desire to be right. Then maybe, at long last, Jesus' own prayer will be answered:

> *"That all of them may be one, Father, just as you are in me and I am in you. May they also be in us so that the world may believe that you have sent me. I have given them the glory that you gave me, that they may be one as we are one—I in them and you in me—so that they may be brought to complete unity. Then the world will know that you sent me and have loved them even as you have loved me."* **–John 17:21-22**

CHAPTER 14

The Cost and Reward of Unity

*Q*while back, I moved into a new home with a big, beautiful fireplace. There was only one problem: it was a gas fireplace and gas fireplaces can be expensive to run. This particular complex didn't allow residents to burn wood in the fireplaces, so you had to use the costly gas or go without a fire.

A week or two after I moved in, we had a cold spell and I got to try the fireplace out sooner than expected. Southern California in May does not usually afford great opportunities to gather around a nice cozy fire, so it was a wonderful surprise. I turned the gas on, threw a match into the mix and voila—instant fire! I was very careful, though, to keep the gas at a moderate level.

I enjoyed the fire, but I found myself watching the clock. I didn't want to let it burn any longer than necessary. I wanted the fire, but I also didn't want it to cost too much. I ended up having a lovely evening, but it was dampened significantly by my concern for the potential expense. My concern for the cost kept me from being able to fully lose myself in the moment.

Ultimately, I ended up shutting it down altogether — probably far sooner than was really necessary.

You may know where I'm going with this, but I needed a little help. A night or two later, as I was in that twilight stage between sleeping and waking, I had a dream. I was lying on the floor enjoying a nice little fire in my beautiful new fireplace. A man came into the room and walked over to the valve that controls the gas and promptly turned it all the way up. Immediately the fireplace burst into an all-consuming display of color, warmth, and radiance. I was stunned to realize that until that moment I hadn't even been aware that it *could* burn so much brighter. I was captivated by the fire and not at all afraid that the flames could not be contained within the safety of the fireplace. But then I had a thought — *what was it going to cost?* Surely turning the gas up that high would be expensive. I became so alarmed about the cost, that before I even knew what I was doing, I reached out and turned the gas back down. Immediately, the flames died down and it reverted back to my nice, safe, less costly, fire. I thought to myself, *this isn't so bad, and it's much more affordable.*

It doesn't take a lot of prophetic insight to interpret my dream. It also isn't difficult to imagine that most of us — *often without even realizing it* — have put our hands on what God is doing in an attempt to keep the fire at a nice, manageable level. The fire of God *is* majestic and beautiful, so much more glorious than we even know, but he is an *all consuming fire*. We can't enter *that* fire and expect to keep everything contained within our safe, orderly little existence. If we want the fire of God, we need to understand there is a very real cost.

The All Consuming Fire of His Presence

If we ever want to see that all consuming display of his glory and splendor, we need to figure out how badly we really want him. We are so satisfied with so little. So much so that I am convinced we're not even aware of how little we really have.

I don't ever intentionally want to turn down the fire, but I probably have more often, and in more ways, than I've ever realized. I know I'm not alone. Sometimes, in his mercy, the Lord has even turned the fire down for me. In my well intended but occasionally misguided zeal, I've often asked for a revelation of his glory and holiness beyond my current ability to bear. Fire either destroys or it purifies — it all depends on what goes into the fire.

There *is* a cost for living in his presence. To be clear, I'm not referring to the normal trials of life that come from living in a fallen world. We all experience various troubles and heartaches throughout our lives and we need to be secure enough in Christ that our faith is not constantly shaken by the cares of the world (which will always be with us). *The cost I'm referring to is the price of dwelling in the very center of the flames.*

It is subjecting ourselves to holiness that is unrelenting in its revelation of our flawed character and brokenness. It is being so consumed with who he is and what he desires, that we would do anything and go anywhere to satisfy the longing of his heart. It is letting down the protective barriers in our hearts so we can love what he loves and hate what he hates. It is allowing our hearts to be broken by the things that break his. It is moving far beyond our little ministries and little dreams and moving into the dreams of God. It is places of encounter that change everything. It is a lot more of God than will fit into any religious box we've ever tried to confine him to. It is being so deeply consumed with passion for Jesus, the glorious burning Man, that our only remaining desire is to be where he is and do what he does.

I'm not there yet—not even close. It's much easier to write the words than it is to live them. *But I want to be there.* I want him to be all that's on my mind, all the time. I want to be consumed by his heart and his passion. I want to be so captivated by the fire in his eyes, that though I've counted the cost, I look at him and say, "Cost? What cost?" I want to live my life from the very center of the flames and I don't *ever* want to reach out extinguish any part of that blaze again!

On a corporate basis, we are only too ready to extinguish the blaze. One of the great travesties of our modern western church culture is that we are so accustomed to "turning down the fire" that most of what happens in our gatherings on any given week happens with little to no involvement of the Holy Spirit. The glory has departed and most haven't even noticed. We are like the lukewarm church of Laodicea—Jesus himself is standing outside knocking and we haven't yet invited him in.

But thankfully this is only a part of the current picture. Even now, there are many sincere seekers—from churches of every shape, size, and variety—who *are* beginning to hear his knock on the door of their hearts. They are beginning to hear his call. They are beginning to sense a stirring. There is a growing hunger in their hearts for more. They are the ones, like the Shulamite in the Song of Solomon, who are fervently searching for their Beloved, *"Have you seen the one my heart loves?"* (Song of Solomon 3:3). Deep is calling out to deep, beckoning us to return to our First Love.

The call, of course, originates in the heart of God himself. Jesus said the greatest commandment is to *"Love the Lord your God with all your heart and with all your soul and with all your mind."* He went on to add, *"And the second is like it: Love your neighbor as yourself"* (Matthew 22:37, 39). It is in returning to the simplicity of loving God with all of our heart, soul, and mind—

and then loving each other out of the overflow — that we return to the only true basis for unity.

The Anointing of Unity

Some years ago, while reading the story of the Woman at the Well, I was struck by the importance and impact of a *single* encounter with Jesus. In a single encounter with Jesus, the Samaritan woman's life was completely changed. I know that my own love for Jesus was not birthed out of a good message, a good book, or from observing someone else's sincere life of devotion. While those things are enormously helpful, and even necessary, *I have been transformed in his presence.* I can't help but believe it is only a greater corporate revelation of his presence that will lead to a greater corporate transformation. We will always have choices as to how we respond to his presence individually, but until we learn to host his presence in our *corporate* gatherings, many will never see a true outpouring of his Spirit.

There is a genuine hunger and thirst growing among the people of God for what is real. Increasing numbers are fed up with the status quo and long for a fresh and genuine encounter with the Ancient of Days. In the first chapter, I mentioned that we are not usually willing to change until the pain of staying the same becomes greater than the pain of change. I think we are reaching that point. Our world is changing. We have not overcome evil with good, we are allowing evil to overcome us. Without the purifying and healing fire of his presence, the body of Christ remains broken, weak, and fragmented. And a broken, weak, and sick body will never have a significant positive impact on a broken, weak, and sick world.

We were not created to be broken and fragmented, we were created to be healed and whole. What would happen if we heeded the words of Paul and matured into the full stature of our intended purpose? *"In all things grow up into him who is the Head, that is, Christ"* (Ephesians 4:15). If the body *was* healed and whole—rightly related to the Head—what impact would we have on the world around us? I think Psalm 133 gives us a hint of what *that* would look like:

> *How good and pleasant it is when brothers live together in unity! It is like precious oil poured on the head, running down on Aaron's beard, down upon the collar of his robes. It is as if the dew of Hermon were falling on Mount Zion. For there the LORD bestows his blessing, even life forevermore.*
> **–Psalm 133:1-3**

There is a level of corporate anointing reserved for a Church walking in unity. The anointing flows down from the head onto a single, whole body. Once it starts to flow from the head, it builds momentum that brings life and blessing forevermore!

There is a great battle taking place over this very issue. The strategy of hell to kill, steal and destroy—and to divide, separate and weaken—is still very much at work. "Every kingdom divided against itself will be ruined, and every city or household divided against itself will not stand" (Matthew 12:25). Yet together—each part in place—we invite a flow of the oil of heaven that not only flows over us, but also off of us onto a dry and thirsty world.

It's interesting that the anointing oil flows first from the head. Of course Christ is the Head of the Church and all genuine anointing flows from him. But I think this is also a reminder that the oil of his Spirit needs to first touch our minds and our thoughts before it can flow to the rest of the body. In our quick judgment of others—like James and John who wanted to call fire down from heaven on the Samaritans when they didn't welcome Jesus (see Luke 9:54-56) — we often "don't know what kind of spirit we are of" simply because we have failed to take our thoughts captive to the obedience of Christ. We need to be "transformed by the renewing of our minds"(Romans 12:2 paraphrased) and align our minds with God's perfect will, before true cohesiveness can occur in the body.

From the head and over the beard, the oil then flows down onto the robe. I was praying for the Church recently, both local and global, and I saw a picture of the bride in an old, soiled robe. She wanted to put on new clean and pure garments, but the zipper on the old garment was rusted and stuck. Then I saw the oil of his Spirit come and "lubricate" the zipper. Once the zipper was made functional again by the anointing of the Holy Spirit, she was able to take off the old, soiled robe and put on a new and beautiful pure white robe. Oh, how we need the presence of the Holy Spirit to wash over us and clothe us in new, clean garments of purity and love!

Truly it *is* "good and pleasant" for brothers to dwell together in unity. Not only will we walk in a new level of anointing as we learn to walk in the virtue of love "which binds them all together in perfect unity" (Colossian 3:14), there is also a new level of peace and joy that comes only from the satisfaction of being rightly related to him and each other. Yet as much as I long to know this reality for our sakes — and especially for the sakes of those who have yet to see an authentic representation of his love — it is not the primary motivation of my heart. More than anything, I continue to long for a healthy, whole body, so Jesus will have *his* reward. Until we are finally able to "lay hold of that for which he laid hold of us" (Phil 3:12 paraphrased), he won't have the fullness of his heart's desire.

The Reward of His Suffering

In the 1700's, two Moravians missionaries sold themselves into slavery for the sake of the gospel. It was the only way they knew to reach other slaves in the West Indies with the good news of God's love and salvation. As the slave ship sailed away, they shouted, *"May the Lamb that was slain receive the reward of his suffering!"*

From the very first time I heard this quote, it had, and continues to have, a profound impact on my heart. If we are ever to mature into the unity of faith, our motive for that unity must be more about what it means to *him* than about what it means to us.

Most sincere believers who have trusted Jesus for their eternal redemption, *do* desire to bring God glory. We desire to serve him sincerely. We want our lives to be pleasing to him. But for many, wearied by the cares of life or ensnared by the schemes of hell, somewhere along the way it becomes more about our desires than his. Many start out zealous for God, but their motives end up compromised—and sometimes even replaced—by zeal for results, identity, recognition, purpose, success, or any one of dozens of other lesser pursuits. For others, their own unfulfilled needs and desires choke out their love for the Lord and some stop serving him altogether.

At the risk of sounding like a broken record, I know of only one antidote—a face-to-face encounter with the Living God. It is the fiery gaze of love in his eyes that marks our hearts and ruins us for the ordinary. It is touching the love and passion in his heart that ignites the fire in our own. It is the burning zeal of his jealous jealousy that brands our hearts and keeps us returning to our First Love through every season of life. It's glimpsing the "more" that keeps us from settling for less. When we get a true glimpse of the big picture and taste the dream *in God's heart,* our plans and schemes begin to look so small and shallow. And the *"momentary light afflictions"* we experience on this planet are put in their right perspective as we await *"an eternal glory that far outweighs them all"* (2 Cor. 4:17).

After a time of personal loss, Isaiah's zeal was renewed and he was given a new assignment *after* he got a fresh glimpse of God's glory (see Isaiah 6). While in God's presence, Isaiah overheard a cry that is always in God's heart: *"Who will go for us, whom shall I send?"* Isaiah was revived when he saw the Lord and heard the cry of God's heart — *then* he was sent with a very specific message for a specific group of people. Because Isaiah was sent directly from the throne of God, he became a partner in fulfilling the very dreams of heaven.

God isn't just looking for those who will go, he is looking for those he can *send* with his own heart. Yet what that looks like for me and what that looks like for you, may be *very* different things. He may send us around the world or across the street. He may send us out to teach Sunday school or to teach the multitudes. He may send us to minister to his people in acts of service, or to minister to his own heart in acts of worship. As long as we're moving with him, the "what" doesn't matter so much. What matters far more is the "why."

We don't go in an attempt to "save the world" — or to accomplish any other specific goal for that matter — we go to fulfill *our* role in satisfying the longing of our Bridegroom's heart. When our focus is on being faithful stewards of what he has specifically entrusted to us — rather than on achieving a particular measure of earthly success — *we will never fail.*

The key is to move *with him* — to dance to the rhythm of his heart. Whether the dance is fast or slow; whether it is moving forward or moving in circles; whether it is moving to the right or to the left—he is looking for those who will *move with him wherever he goes.* In Luke 10:1, Jesus sent the disciples out ahead of him—to the places *"he was about to go."* How do you know where Jesus is about to go? You stay close enough to hear his heart. When you remain rightly related to him—in a place of abiding and intimate communion—you are able to go where he goes and do what you see him doing.

A father will often give his young child chores to help train him. A master expects a slave to do what they are told because that is their role. But *a husband* wants a bride who will move in partnership with him. This is what our God wants. A mature bride who has "made herself ready" will function quite differently than a child who is learning to do simple chores, or a servant who merely follows orders.

During a recent time of prayer, I saw myself taking a leisurely stroll with Jesus through an amazing, lush garden. Eventually we headed up a path that led to magnificent arched entry—ornate double doors opened for us before we even reached them. We entered and walked down a corridor that seemed to go on forever. Scores of angels lowered their wings and bowed in reverence as we passed. Finally, we reached the royal throne room—the place of his dwelling. It was beautiful beyond description! Clearly, there was only One worthy to sit upon *this* throne. He took his rightful place and instinctively I fell to my knees. As I bowed low before him, unashamed tears of love and gratitude began to flow freely. I wanted to kiss his feet and never stop. My heart longed to worship him in this place forever. But abruptly, he interrupted me. He took my hand and gently lifted me to my feet. Then he did something completely unexpected. Something shocking! He motioned for me to sit beside him—*on his own throne!*

Knowing my apprehension, he reminded me that unlike the angels who worship him ceaselessly, I was created in his own image. Although he loves and accepts my worship, he cherishes my intimate friendship and partnership even more. His specific word to me was that he didn't shed his blood just so I could sit at his feet—he shed his blood so I could sit down *beside* him.

> *"To him who overcomes, I will give the right to sit with me on my throne, just as I overcame and sat down with my Father on his throne."* **–Rev 3:21**

It is my unfathomable privilege to bow low before him in worship. We will have the blessed honor of singing his praises together, with one voice, for all of eternity. But it is his desire— and his long awaited reward—to have an overcoming and victorious bride who will sit *with him* on his throne.

> *"Father, I want those you have given me to be with me where I am, and to see my glory, the glory you have given me because you loved me before the creation of the world"* **–John 17:24**

This is *his* prayer. This is *his* desire. Even now he wants us to be where he is—to tap into our present-tense reality of being seated with him in heavenly realms—to live and move and breathe in him. His desire is that we lean in so close that we effortlessly move to the rhythm of his heart.

The Lord desires this oneness with each of us individually, and with all of us collectively. He is *still* longing for his bride and she will not be complete until each and every one of us takes our place—every tribe, every tongue, every nation— moving in harmony with him. Each representing a facet of his character; each representing a piece of his heart.

Yes, there is a cost. Experiencing the unrestrained blaze of his glory requires the courage to move out of our comfort zone and into the unknown. It requires the courage to give up lesser passions and the illusion of control. We must be rooted and grounded in love. We must have our identity firmly established in the truth. We must be willing to embrace mystery. We must trust the Holy Spirit in ourselves and in each other. We must daily position ourselves near enough to hear his heart for our own lives, for each other, and for those who have yet to taste the reality of his love. It won't be easy, but it *will* be worth it.

"That they may be one." Could this be the very deepest cry of his heart? From the very beginning, could *this* be the dream he's had in mind? That each and every one of those predestined before the foundations of the world *will* be one? That his bride will be complete — dwelling in oneness with him *and* with each other?

I'm convinced that it is. Because only then will the Spirit and the bride finally join together *in perfect unity* to issue the simple invitation our Bridegroom has long ached to hear:

"Come!"

And only then will the Everlasting Father — who alone knows the day and hour — finally lean over the banister of eternity and issue the decree of the ages. In a single moment, the groaning and longing of creation will cease, and our spirits will leap and unite as the God of glory thunders:

At long last, it is time! Son, go get your bride!

"Even so, come Lord Jesus!"

IV. "CONTINUING TO MAKE HIM KNOWN"

"Righteous Father, though the world does not know you, I know you, and they know that you have sent me. I have made you known to them, and will continue to make you known in order that the love you have for me may be in them and that I myself may be in them."
–John 17:25

𝒯he glorious day of his appearing *will* come. And on that day, we will be one *and* we will be ready. The day of his return for a pure spotless bride is nearer than ever before. We draw closer each and every day, and with each and every breath. But if you are reading these words, most likely today is not that day. We are still here for a reason. We've been given the charge to "occupy" until he comes. As Jesus made the Father known to us, we are to continue to make Jesus known to a lost and hurting world. He is the answer. He is the prize. He is our hope. He is, and forever will be, all we need.

Lord, help us to continue to make you known. As the Father loved you, you have loved us. Let us love the way you love – until Love leads us home.

ABOUT THE AUTHOR

Cindy Powell desires to live her life with one simple focus: Love God and love people. Whether in writing or speaking, her desire is that her words will draw others closer to the heart of God.

Visit her blog and website at:
www.cindypowell.org

Or email: simplefaith247@ gmail.com